foolproof

Jennifer Clouston

Flower Embroidery

Add Texture, Color & Sparkle to Your Organic Garden

80 Stitches & 400 Combinations in a Variety of Fibers

C&T PUBLISHING

Text copyright © 2021 by Jennifer Clouston

Photography and artwork copyright © 2021 by C&T Publishing, Inc.

Publisher: Amy Barrett-Daffin

Creative Director: Gailen Runge

Acquisitions Editor: Roxane Cerda

Managing Editor: Liz Aneloski

Editor: Kathryn Patterson

Technical Editor: Debbie Rodgers

Cover/Book Designer: April Mostek

Production Coordinators: Tim Manibusan and Zinnia Heinzmann

Production Editor: Alice Mace Nakanishi

Illustrator: Mary E. Flynn

Photo Assistant: Lauren Herberg

Photography by Estefany Gonzalez of C&T Publishing, Inc., unless otherwise noted

Published by C&T Publishing, Inc., P.O. Box 1456, Lafayette, CA 94549

Library of Congress Cataloging-in-Publication Data

Names: Clouston, Jennifer, 1959- author.

Title: Foolproof flower embroidery : 80 stitches & 400 combinations in a variety of fibers / Jennifer Clouston.

Description: Lafayette, CA : C&T Publishing, [2021] | "Add texture, color & sparkle to your organic garden." | Includes bibliographical references.

Identifiers: LCCN 2020055426 | ISBN 9781617459740 (trade paperback) | ISBN 9781617459757 (ebook)

Subjects: LCSH: Embroidery. | Decoration and ornament--Plant forms.

Classification: LCC TT773 .C59 2021 | DDC 746.44--dc23

LC record available at https://lccn.loc.gov/2020055426

Printed in the USA

10 9 8

Dedication

To my beloved mother, Penelope Snashall

"In search of my mother's garden, I found my own." —Alice Walker

Snippets and embroidery

Acknowledgments

My husband, Vaughn, your support, time, and above all, your patience are invaluable to me. Once again applying your meticulous attention to detail, your computer skills and drafting all the required illustrations to lay the foundations for C&T Publishing to bring our third book to life. This book is as much yours as it is mine.

A huge thank-you to the team at C&T Publishing—Liz, Roxane, Amy, Gailen, Kathryn, Debbie, Mary, Alice, Zinnia, Tim, April, Estefany, and Lauren. It has once again been a pleasure working with you all. I consider it a privilege to have this opportunity to share my love of all things embroidery.

To the students who come to my workshops, you share my passion and enrich my life.

Contents

CHAPTER 10
Embroidery Stitches...... 67

Gallery 88

Bibliography/
About the Author 95

Introduction

Fabric collage and embroidery

"Start where you are and use what you have" is a mantra that I use when approaching my own work and that of the students in my workshops. As embroiderers and creators, we often follow a pattern. When we see a stitch done in a certain thread that we do not have on hand, we rush out to purchase it or wait days for the thread to arrive in the mail. Creativity simply stops at this point. I encourage you to look beyond the prescribed thread and experiment with those that you have on hand. It is my belief that a large amount of our creativity and uniqueness is lost when we blindly follow a pattern. This extends beyond thread; a stem stitch is not the only stitch that can be used as the stem of a flower, repurposed fabrics can replace new, audition colors that challenge the status quo. Stray off your beaten path; stitch a part of yourself into your embroidery. Play! I dare you!

My goal in this book is to promote creativity and not consumerism. To provide a workbook of various stitches and threads to create all things floral; stems, leaves, petals, centers, and interesting twig effects. I am hoping that this book will inspire a more organic approach to your embroidery, one of creating with the resources that you have in front of you, and freeing yourself from the assumption that if you do not have the "correct" thread your work will not "work."

"I invent nothing, I rediscover."
—Auguste Rodin

How to Use This Book

Design and stitch your own floral embroidery creation.

Stage One

Create the background (page 14) for your floral embroidery.

Place your thread selection onto your chosen background. You may need to add some light and shade to the palette to create dimension and interest.

We will roughly follow the rule-of-thirds composition to draw the stems and main flower heads. Divide the design area into thirds. Sketch the stems and flower heads onto the background fabric ensuring that they are not in the center of the design area.

Select the stitch and thread that you would like to use for the stems (page 19). Stitch the stems as desired.

Next add the centers of the flowers (page 51). The main flower heads do not need to be the same size or shape. Keep this in mind when stitching the centers.

Add the petals (page 31) or create your own petal combination (page 50) to add to the flower centers.

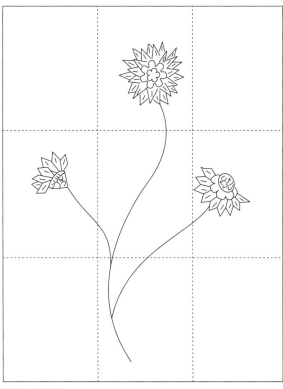

Rule of thirds

Stage One

Stage Two

It's time to add the leaves (page 23) to the design. Start at the bottom of the stem, creating the larger leaves, and work your way up the stem, making the leaves smaller as you go.

Stage Two

Stage Three

Sweet little buds (page 54) are next on the to-do list. Ensure that the buds do not overpower the points of interest, essentially, the main flower heads.

Stage Three

Stage Four

Creating twigs (page 57) is my absolute favorite stage of the design process. Twigs add softening and movement to the floral design. Have fun with them but keep the twigs delicate; using a finer thread will help with this.

Voilà!

You have designed and created your very own original piece of floral embroidery.

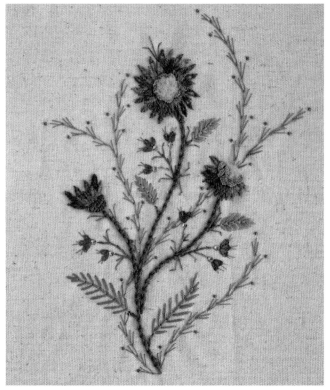

Stage Four

Tools of My Trade

Cutting Tools

A small sharp pair of embroidery scissors and a thread cutter ring are essential. I wear my thread cutter ring on my thumb; it's much more convenient for me than constantly picking up a pair of scissors.

Embroidery Hoops in Various Sizes

Whenever possible I use a hoop to keep my work flat and taught. Because I "stab" my stitches, working in a hoop is a must for this technique of stitching. The flat surface of the fabric in a hoop is more conducive to evenly sized stitches.

Embroidery hoop and pincushion

Fabric Stabilizer

It goes without saying that fabric needs to be stabilized to create evenly formed stitches. A nonwoven iron-on fabric stabilizer does not distort the integrity of the base fabric; linen will still look and feel like linen with a nonwoven stabilizer. ParLan is a low-loft iron-on batting that does not beard and gives a denser feel than a nonwoven stabilizer, which is perfect for bags and purses. If ParLan is not available, Pellon 987F Fusible Fleece has a slightly higher loft and is available at most stores. Additionally, a lovely worn flannel sheet makes for a perfect stabilizer.

Temporary Adhesive

I am not a fan of pinning; threads get tangled in pins and they distort fabric. My solution is to use temporary adhesive spray glue. It holds tiny bits of fabric in place for boro work and when assembling a fabric collage. Odif 505 Spray and Fix Temporary Fabric Adhesive is acid-free, water-soluble, and gentle on fabrics.

Small Hair Iron

Keep a small hair-straightening flat iron nearby to rid silk ribbon of creases and to relax the fibers of Brazilian and other rayon threads.

Tools of my trade

Marking Pens and Pencils

I prefer *not* to use any pen or marker that promises to fade or disappear with heat or water. Bohin has a great chalk pencil that works well on most fabrics, especially wool and felt. The Sewline Trio is a mechanical pencil, with different lead color choices, that creates a fine line and is also erasable. Take the time to investigate any form of marking pen or pencil that you choose to use.

Needles

"The correct size needle is vital to successful embroidery.
Choose a needle appropriately sized to your thread;
this not only makes for easier threading
but also allows the thread to not unravel and
bunch as it passes through the fabric."
—Erica Wilson's Embroidery Book

When it comes to needles, I like to keep things simple. I use only two types of needles: chenille and milliners. I do have a preference to the brand of needles, Bohin being my favorite.

Chenille #22 Needles

- A fat, short needle with a large eye. Perfect for easy threading, it can be your go-to needle for most threads but not for all embroidery stitches.

- It is the only needle to be used with silk ribbon, no matter which stitch.

- Working with metallic threads is much easier using a chenille needle.

- The perfect needle for crewel yarn and wool threads.

- A must for silk perle thread or any other delicate threads. The thickness of the chenille needle and eye creates a clear opening in the fabric for the thickness of the thread to pass through, minimizing the stress on the delicate fibers.

- Great needles for boro work when creating backgrounds.

- As a "stab stitcher," I find the short length of the chenille needle easier to turn and stab up and down in my hoop.

Embroidered pincushion with needles

Milliners/Straw #1, #3, and #9 Needles

- A long, elegant needle with a small eye, the eye being the same size as the shaft of the needle.

- This needle is a must when executing any knots or needle-weaving stitches, such as colonial knots, bullion, and cast-on stitches.

- The milliners #9 needle is small enough to go through most beads.

- The milliners #1 needle is large enough to take all 6 strands of floss or any thicker thread when doing needle weaving, colonial knots, and bullion stitches.

Threads

I have listed the threads that are mostly commonly available. However, as long as the yarn or thread you choose can be threaded through the eye of the needle and travel through the layers of fabric, consider it a thread!

Variety of silk ribbon and threads

There are more threads on the market than we know what to do with. I prefer to work with what I have on hand, either from my stash, thrift stores, hand-me-downs from friends, or purchased from my local quilt stores.

Stranded Cotton or Floss

We all have more of this most common thread than we will use in a lifetime! It is however, my least favorite thread to use. It is great (all 6 strands) for needle weaving, knots, and dimensional embroidery. A single strand is ideal for stamens, fine twigs, and branches. However, stranded cotton was manufactured to separate and that is exactly what it does. Try not to use stranded cotton when "traveling" with a stitch.

Perle #16, #12, #8, #5, and #3

This is the thread that I use most frequently. It is tightly twisted and versatile. Brands such as Valdani, Cottage Garden Threads, and Chameleon Threads come in a wonderful range of colors, both variegated and solid.

Crewel Wool

This is a two-ply wool used predominantly in crewel embroidery. I find working with this thread to be very relaxing. It is important to work a looser tension when working with a wool thread; see Threading Crewel Wool (page 66).

Crochet Cotton

This is a twisted thread very similar in appearance and texture to perle thread and it comes in a variety of thicknesses.

Tapestry Wool

These threads are very useful when adding dimension and texture and are often found in abundance at thrift stores.

Twisted Silk

This thread is simply luscious. Working with this thread is a delight; the colors are vibrant with a beautiful sheen to them. Use a chenille #22 needle to preserve the delicate fibers. Colour Streams has a wide variety of colors available.

Metallic Thread

For a bit of bling, I use metallic threads. Use them sparingly to throw light and to create dimension. Always use a chenille #22 needle and a thread conditioner to help settle those prickly fibers.

Silk Ribbon: 2mm, 4mm, and 7mm

Be still my beating heart! Silk ribbon embroidery is instant gratification embroidery. It comes in a variety of colors both variegated and solid. Silk ribbon embroidery effortlessly fills a space. It is paramount to use a chenille #22 needle and to have "soft hands" when working with silk ribbon; see How to Start and Stop with Silk Ribbon (page 66). Use a hand-held flat iron (page 10) to quickly rid silk ribbon of any creases.

EdMar Rayon Thread

There are a few rules to follow when working with this dynamic and strong thread. First, never split the plies and always try to use a hoop. Rayon threads most certainly have a "right" and "wrong" end to thread; see Threading Brazilian Threads (page 66). When knotting threads (page 65) or ending off threads (page 65), make knots small and secure. Always work from left to right and wrap the thread around the needle (for bullion knots and such) clockwise. Bullion and cast-on stitches should be wrapped loosely; always use a milliners #1 needle. To relax the fibers gently press with a fabric iron or hand-held flat iron (page 10).

Nymo Beading Thread

This is the perfect beading thread as it does not stretch over time. There is nothing worse than a wobbly bead! Nymo thread is available in a large variety of colors. Always match the color of the thread to the bead.

Specialty Threads

Satin floss (by DMC), tulle threads or ribbons, needlepoint ribbon (Neon Rays, Very Velvet, and others by Rainbow Gallery)—all these diverse threads add an eclectic and interesting touch to your embroidery.

Bits and Bobs

Buttons, lace, beads, and yarn

Buttons, beads, sequins, lace, and yarn all add dimension to your embroidery. Textured yarn can be couched down to create trunks and branches of trees, buttons and beads replace colonial knots for centers of flowers, and lace adds dimension to background fabrics. Felt cut into shapes such as petals and leaves adds interest to floral embroidery.

Embroidery with felt, sequins, and beads

2 Creating Backgrounds

My mantra, "Start where you are and use what you have," is a very strong motivator when choosing backgrounds for my embroidery. I have a penchant for preloved fabrics, such as vintage or antique fabrics, tablecloths, and thrift store finds. When working with vintage or preloved fabric, it is important that you soak or wash it to remove stains.

As a quilter, my fabric stash and uncompleted projects are also valuable sources of backgrounds.

Whether I am using a single layer of fabric, a patchwork or crazy-quilt block, a collage, or a piece of boro work, I *always* use a fabric stabilizer.

Vintage fabrics, orphan blocks, repurposed fabrics, and clothing

A Single Piece of Fabric

Cut the fabric and stabilizer to the desired size. Press the fabric well and fuse the stabilizer of choice to the wrong side of the fabric.

Crazy-Quilt Block

Foundation Method

1. Cut the foundation fabric and stabilizer to the desired size. Press the foundation fabric well.

2. Cut a five-sided piece of fabric and place right side up in the center of the foundation fabric.

> **NOTE**
> It is important to note that a generous ½″ (12mm) seam allowance is needed in this method of piecing.

3. Cut a rectangle of a different fabric. Lay this second patch along one of the edges of the first piece with right sides together.

4. Sew the second piece of fabric in place along the edge and flip over to reveal the right side of the fabric. Press well.

5. Continue in this manner until the desired size has been reached.

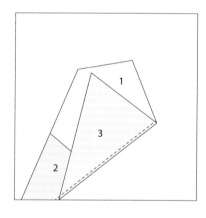

6. Sew along the perimeter of the block within the seam allowance.

7. Press well and fuse the stabilizer of choice to the wrong side of the block.

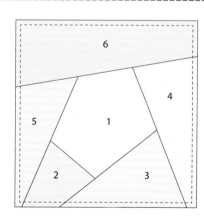

Boro Work

The Japanese word *boro* is literally translated as scraps of cloth or rags. The word is also used to describe clothing or household items which have been patched and repaired with small pieces of fabric many times over many years.

Technically, it is a utilitarian form of hand sewing that uses a simple running stitch (Sashiko) that pierces through several layers of fabric, securing the fabric scraps.

1. Cut the foundation fabric and stabilizer to the desired size. Press the foundation fabric well and fuse the stabilizer of choice to the wrong side of the fabric.

2. Arrange fabric scraps onto the foundation fabric, overlapping them by a healthy ¼″ (6mm). You might find it useful to glue the shapes down as you go.

3. Using Sashiko thread or a thread of choice, stitch across the width of the piece of foundation fabric. It is important to leave a loop of thread at each end when changing direction.

Boro work with embroidery

Boro work with loops of thread created when turning

Snippets Background

Snippets collage

This is a fun way to use up the tiniest pieces of fabric and lace.

1. Cut the pieces of foundation fabric and stabilizer to the desired size, allowing a little extra for shrinkage.

2. Fuse the stabilizer onto the wrong side of the background fabric.

3. Lay the snippets of fabric and lace onto the foundation fabric, overlapping each other so no part of the foundation fabric is visible. Spray glue or baste in place.

4. Secure the snippets onto the foundation fabric with a matching thread using a "working" stitch, such as herringbone, blanket, or running stitch.

Secure snippets onto foundation fabric with working stitches.

Fabric Collage

Fabric collage

The fabric collage technique is very similar to that of "snippets."

1. Cut the pieces of foundation fabric and stabilizer to the desired size. Fuse the stabilizer onto the wrong side of the background fabric.

2. Lay the scraps of fabric and lace onto the foundation fabric, overlapping each other so no part of the foundation fabric is visible. The frayed and raw edges of fabric add texture and interest to collage work. Spray glue or baste the fabric pieces in place.

3. Add a combination of working stitches (herringbone, blanket, hem, or running stitches) and embroidered flowers to secure the raw edges of the fabric scraps in place. Once all the embroidery is completed, remove the basting stitches.

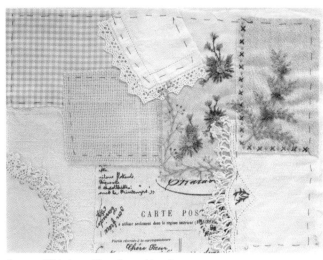

Scraps of fabric and lace basted in place

Patchwork Blocks

Press a completed patchwork block well and fuse fabric stabilizer to the wrong side.

Orphan blocks and vintage patchwork blocks

Repurposed Clothing

Make sure that the repurposed clothing is clean and free from stains. Unpick the garments along the seams. The pockets and button fronts are a valuable source of interest to your embroidery projects.

Fuse the stabilizer of choice to the wrong side of the fabric.

Repurposed clothing with pocket intact

Mixed Textile Weaving

Inspired by the incredibly talented Jude Hill, weaving with cloth creates an interesting and textured background suitable for embroidery.

1. Cut the foundation fabric to the desired size and place onto a flat working surface.

2. Cut or rip the fabrics and lace.

3. Lay the vertical strips of fabric and lace edge to edge onto the foundation fabric.

4. Basket weave the horizontal strips of fabric through the vertical strips.

5. Baste the strips in place and embroider as desired.

Mixed textile weaving

3 | Embroidery Stitches for Stems

Stems hold up the flower heads but should not dominate the design. The stitch and color of the stems should be determined by the background of choice.

STEMS *one*

A	Straight feather stitch (page 83) • *Metallic thread*	**L**	Couching (page 74) • *Metallic thread*
B	Rope stitch (page 81) • *EdMar Lola*	**M**	Beaded fly stitch (page 68) • *Nymo thread, beads*
C	Feather stitch (page 76) • *Crewel wool*	**N**	Palestrina knot stitch (page 80) • *Crewel wool*
D	Rope stitch (page 81) • *Crewel wool*	**O**	Palestrina knot stitch (page 80) • *Crochet cotton*
E	Feather stitch (page 76), Whipping stitch (page 86) • *Crochet cotton*	**P**	Couching (page 74) • *Tapestry wool*
		Q	Couching (page 74) • *Crochet cotton*
F	Fern stitch (page 77) • *Crewel wool*	**R**	Couching (page 74) • *Knitting yarn*
G	Palestrina knot stitch (page 80) • *Perle #8*	**S**	Beaded backstitch (page 67) • *Nymo thread, beads*
H	Fern stitch (page 77) • *2mm silk ribbon*	**T**	Beaded backstitch (page 67) • *Nymo thread, beads*
I	Backstitch (page 67), Straight stitch (page 83) • *Twisted silk*	**U**	Beaded feather stitch (page 68) • *Nymo thread, beads*
J	Backstitch (page 67) • *Perle #5*; Whipping stitch (page 86) • *Crewel wool*	**V**	Beaded backstitch (page 67) • *Nymo thread, beads*
		W	Beaded fly stitch (page 68) • *Nymo thread, beads*
K	Backstitch (page 67) • *Tapestry wool*		

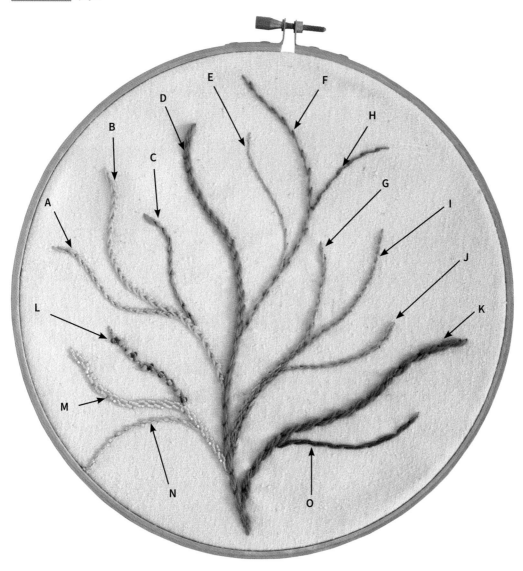

A Portuguese knotted stem stitch (page 80) • *Perle #8*

B Portuguese knotted stem stitch (page 80) • *Crochet cotton*

C Portuguese knotted stem stitch (page 80) • *2mm silk ribbon*

D Stem stitch (page 83) • *Tapestry yarn*

E Thin stem stitch (page 83) • *Twisted silk*

F Thin stem stitch (page 83) • *Crewel wool*

G Stem stitch (page 83) • *Crewel wool, metallic thread*

H Thin stem stitch (page 83) • *Perle #8*

I Stem stitch (page 83) • *Crewel wool*

J Stem stitch (page 83) • *Crewel wool, twisted silk*

K Alternating stem stitch (page 67) • *Tapestry wool*

L Stem stitch with beads (page 83) • *Perle #8, beads*

M Beaded stem stitch (page 71) • *Nymo thread, beads*

N Stem stitch with beads (page 83) • *Perle #12, beads*

O Alternating stem stitch (page 67) • *Crochet cotton*

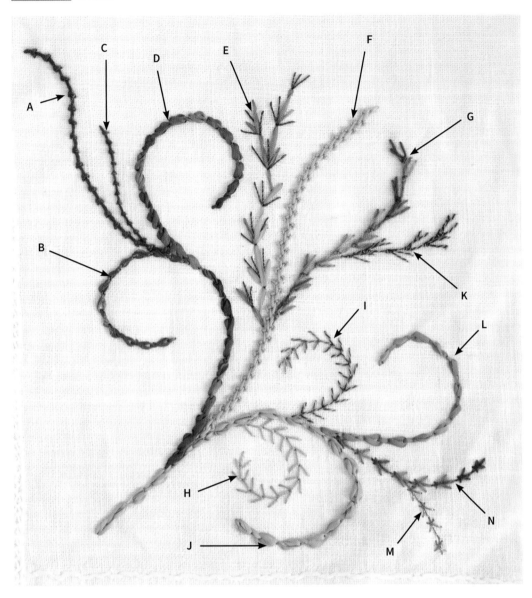

A   Coral stitch (page 74) • *Perle #5*

B   Uneven chain stitch (page 85) • *Needlepoint ribbon*

C   Coral stitch (page 74) • *Perle #8*

D   Uneven chain stitch (page 85) • *4mm silk ribbon*

E   Straight stitch (page 83) • *2mm silk ribbon, EdMar Frost*

F   Spanish knotted feather stitch (page 82) • *Crochet cotton*

G   Feather twig stitch (page 76) • *Crewel wool*

H   Fly stitch (page 78) • *Perle #8*

I   Fly stitch (page 78) • *Perle #12*

J   Chain ribbon stitch (page 73) • *4mm silk ribbon*

K   Feather twig stitch (page 76) • *Perle #8*

L   Chain ribbon stitch (page 73) • *2mm silk ribbon*

M   Thorn stitch (page 84) • *Metallic thread*

N   Thorn stitch (page 84) • *Crewel wool*

A Chain feathered stitch (page 73) • *Crochet cotton*

B Chain stitch (page 74) • *Perle #8*; Whipping stitch (page 86) • *Stranded cotton*

C Chain stitch (page 74) • *EdMar Frost*

D Wheatear stitch (page 85) • *Crochet cotton*

E Twisted chain stitch (page 84) • *2mm silk ribbon*

F Twisted chain stitch (page 84) • *Perle #8*

G Chain stitch (page 74), Straight stitch (page 83) • *Crewel wool*

H Chain stitch (page 74), Straight stitch (page 83) • *Perle #8*

I Single twisted chain stitch (page 82) • *Crewel wool*

J Chain stitch (page 74), Backstitch (page 67) • *Perle #8*

Embroidery Stitches for Leaves

What a variety of leaves there are from which to choose! Experiment with threads; two different colors or types of thread on one needle, different shades for each side of one leaf, making the edges of the leaf smooth or uneven. Play!

LEAVES Fishbone Stitch

LEAVES Fishbone Stitch *one*

A	Fishbone stitch: staggered (page 77) • *Crewel wool*
B	Fishbone stitch: staggered (page 77) • *4mm silk ribbon*
C	Fishbone stitch: uneven edge (page 77) • *Very Velvet (by Rainbow Gallery) thread*
D	Fishbone stitch (page 77) • *Tapestry wool*
E	Fishbone stitch (page 77) • *Crewel wool, metallic thread (1 needle)*
F	Fishbone stitch: uneven edge (page 77) • *Crewel wool (2 colors), Nymo thread, beads*
G	Fishbone stitch: uneven edge (page 77) • *Perle #8*
H	Fishbone stitch (page 77) • *4mm silk ribbon*
I	Fishbone stitch: uneven edge (page 77) • *Stranded cotton*
J	Fishbone stitch (page 77) with beads • *Nymo thread, beads*
K	Fishbone stitch: staggered (page 77) with beads • *Nymo thread, beads*
L	Fishbone stitch: open (page 77) • *Needlepoint ribbon*
M	Fishbone stitch: open (page 77) • *Stranded cotton*
N	Fishbone stitch: open (page 77); Backstitch (page 67) • *Needlepoint ribbon*

O	Fishbone stitch: uneven edge (page 77) • *Tapestry wool*
P	Fishbone stitch: open (page 77); Backstitch (page 67) • *Crewel wool*
Q	Fishbone stitch: open (page 77); Backstitch (page 67) • *Perle #8*
R	Fishbone stitch (page 77), Straight stitch (page 83) • *2mm silk ribbon, stranded cotton*

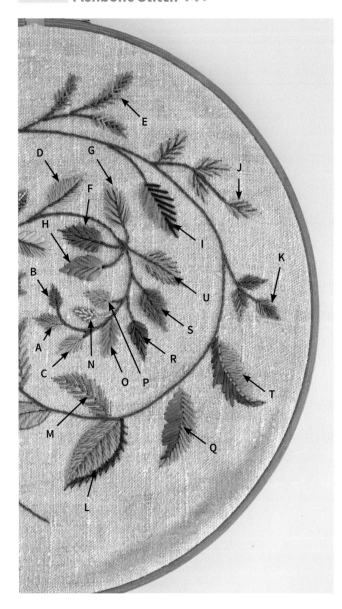

A	Fishbone stitch (page 77) • *EdMar Lola*
B	Fishbone stitch (page 77) • *Perle #8*
C	Fishbone stitch (page 77) • *Stranded cotton*
D	Fishbone stitch (page 77) • *Crewel wool, perle #5*
E	Fishbone stitch: open (page 77) • *Perle #8*
F	Fishbone stitch (page 77) • *Tapestry wool;* Straight stitch (page 83) • *Perle #12*
G	Fishbone stitch (page 77) • *Stranded cotton, crochet thread*
H	Fishbone stitch (page 77) • *4mm silk ribbon*
I	Fishbone stitch: open (page 77) • *Very Velvet (by Rainbow Gallery) thread*
J	Fishbone stitch (page 77), Straight stitch (page 83) • *Crewel wool*
K	Fishbone stitch (page 77) • *Perle #8*
L	Fishbone stitch (page 77), Single twisted chain stitch (page 82), Straight stitch (page 83) • *Crewel wool*
M	Fishbone stitch (page 77) • *Crewel wool, metallic thread, perle #8*
N	Fishbone stitch (page 77) with beads • *Nymo thread, beads*
O	Fishbone stitch (page 77) • *Very Velvet (by Rainbow Gallery) thread*
P	Fishbone stitch (page 77) • *Crewel wool*
Q	Fishbone stitch: uneven edge (page 77) • *Needlepoint ribbon, crewel wool, metallic thread*
R	Fishbone stitch (page 77) • *2mm silk ribbon*
S	Fishbone stitch (page 77) • *Tapestry wool*
T	Fishbone stitch: uneven edge (page 77) • *Crewel wool, 2mm silk ribbon*; Backstitch (page 67) • *Crewel wool*
U	Fishbone stitch (page 77), Straight stitch (page 83) • *Crewel wool*

A Fly stitch (page 78), Backstitch (page 67) • *Perle #8*

B Fly stitch (page 78) • *Tapestry cotton*

C Fly stitch (page 78), Straight stitch (page 83) • *Twisted silk*

D Fly stitch (page 78) • *Metallic thread*

E Fly stitch (page 78) • *Perle #8, perle #12*

F Fly stitch (page 78) • *Crewel wool*

G Fly stitch (page 78) • *2mm silk ribbon*

H Fly stitch (page 78) • *Perle #8*

I Fly stitch (page 78), Stem stitch (page 83) • *Perle #12*; Single bead stitch (page 82) • *Nymo thread, beads*

J Fly stitch (page 78) • *Stranded cotton*

K Beaded fly stitch (page 68) • *Nymo thread, beads*

L Beaded fly stitch (page 68) • *Nymo thread, beads*

M Beaded fly stitch (page 68) • *Nymo thread, beads*

N Fly stitch (page 78), Stem stitch (page 83) • *Crewel wool*

O Fly stitch (page 78), Single twisted chain stitch (page 82) • *Perle #12*

P Fly stitch (page 78) • *Nymo thread, bugle beads, beads*

Q Fly stitch (page 78), Single twisted chain stitch (page 82) • *Perle #8*

R Fly stitch (page 78), Single twisted chain stitch (page 82) • *Metallic thread*

S Fly stitch (page 78) • *Tapestry wool*; Straight stitch (page 83) • *Crewel wool*

T Fly stitch (page 78), Single twisted chain stitch (page 82) • *EdMar Frost*

U Fly stitch (page 78), Single twisted chain stitch (page 82) • *Stranded cotton*

V Fly stitch (page 78), Single twisted chain stitch (page 82) • *Crewel wool*

W Fly stitch (page 78), Single twisted chain stitch (page 82) • *2mm silk ribbon*

X Fly stitch (page 78), Single twisted chain stitch (page 82) • *Tapestry wool*

Y Fly stitch (page 78), Single twisted chain stitch (page 82) • *4mm silk ribbon*

Z Fly stitch (page 78) • *Nymo thread, bugle beads, bead*

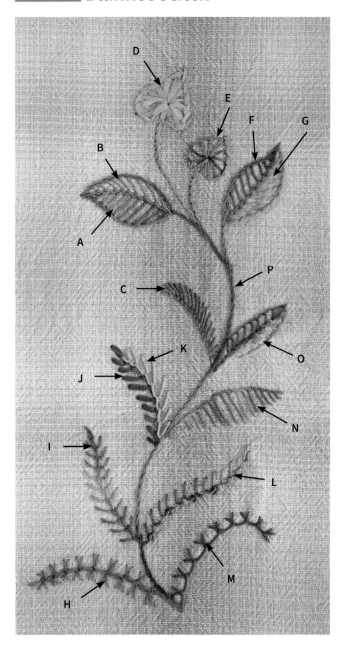

A	Blanket stitch (page 71), Stem stitch (page 83) • *Perle #8*
B	Blanket stitch (page 71) • *Metallic thread*
C	Blanket stitch (page 71) • *Perle #8*
D	Blanket stitch (page 71) • *2mm silk ribbon*
E	Blanket stitch (page 71) • *EdMar Lola*
F	Blanket stitch (page 71), Stem stitch (page 83) • *Perle #8*
G	Blanket stitch (page 71) • *Crewel wool*
H	Up-and-down blanket stitch (page 85) • *Crewel wool*
I	Blanket stitch (page 71) • *Perle #8*
J	Blanket stitch (page 71) • *2mm silk ribbon*
K	Blanket stitch (page 71) • *Crochet cotton*
L	Blanket stitch (page 71) with beads • *Perle #8*
M	Up-and-down blanket stitch (page 85) • *Crochet cotton*
N	Blanket stitch (page 71) • *Perle #8*
O	Blanket stitch (page 71) • *Stranded cotton*
P	Stem stitch (page 83) • *Perle #8*

Lazy Daisy Stitch

A Lazy daisy stitch (page 79) • *Various threads, silk ribbon*

B Lazy daisy stitch (page 79), Colonial knot (page 74) • *Various threads, silk ribbons*

C Knotted lazy daisy stitch (page 79) • *Various threads, silk ribbons*

D Bullion lazy daisy stitch (page 72) • *Various threads, silk ribbons*

E Stem stitch (page 83) • *Perle #12*

F Stem stitch (page 83) • *Stranded cotton*

G Stem stitch (page 83) • *Perle #8*

A
Leaves: Stem stitch (page 83), Lazy daisy stitch (page 79) • *EdMar Lola*
Stem: Chain stitch (page 74), Whipping stitch (page 86) • *EdMar Lola*

B
Leaves: Lazy daisy stitch (page 79) • *7mm silk ribbon*; Straight stitch (page 83) • *Single strand of stranded cotton*
Stem: Stem stitch (page 83) • *Twisted silk*

C
Leaves: Bullion lazy daisy stitch (page 72) • *Crochet cotton, crewel wool*
Stem: Couching (page 74) • *Perle #8*

D
Leaves: Twisted lazy daisy stitch (page 84) • *Assorted threads, silk ribbons*
Stem: Backstitch (page 67) • *Crochet cotton*

E
Leaves: Lazy daisy stitch (page 79) • *Metallic thread, 2mm silk ribbon, perle #8*
Stem: Stem stitch (page 83) • *Metallic thread*; Couching (page 74) • *2mm silk ribbon*

F
Leaves: Lazy daisy stitch (page 79) • *Crewel wool*
Stem: Backstitch (page 67) • *Crewel wool*

G
Leaves: Lazy daisy stitch (page 79) • *Perle #8 (2 colors, 1 needle)*; Beaded lazy daisy stitch (page 69), Beaded pointed petal/leaf (page 70), Single bead stitch (page 82) • *Nymo thread, beads*
Stem: Twisted chain stitch (page 84) • *Perle #8*

H
Leaves: Lazy daisy stitch extended (page 79) • *Assorted threads, silk ribbon*
Stem: Stem stitch (page 83) • *Perle #12*

I
Leaves: Twisted lazy daisy stitch (page 84) • *Perle #12, crochet cotton*
Stem: Stem stitch (page 83) • *Perle #12, crochet cotton*

LEAVES Dimensional Stitches

A	Woven bar (page 86) • *Crochet cotton*
B	Woven bar (page 86) • *Perle #5*
C	Woven bar (page 86) • *Perle #8*
D	Drizzle stitch (page 76) • *EdMar Lola*
E	Drizzle stitch (page 76) • *Crewel wool*
F	Woven picot (page 86) • *Perle #12*
G	Drizzle stitch (page 76) • *Stranded cotton*
H	Drizzle stitch (page 76) • *Perle #12*
I	Drizzle stitch (page 76) • *Perle #8*
J	Drizzle stitch (page 76) • *Crochet cotton*
K	Woven picot (page 86) • *EdMar Frost*
L	Woven picot (page 86) • *Crewel wool*
M	Woven picot (page 86) • *Tapestry cotton*
N	Woven bar (page 86) • *Tapestry wool*
O	Woven bar (page 86) • *Tapestry cotton*
P	Woven bar (page 86) • *Crewel wool*
Q	Woven picot (page 86) • *Perle #8*
R	Palestrina knot stitch (page 80) • *Crochet cotton*

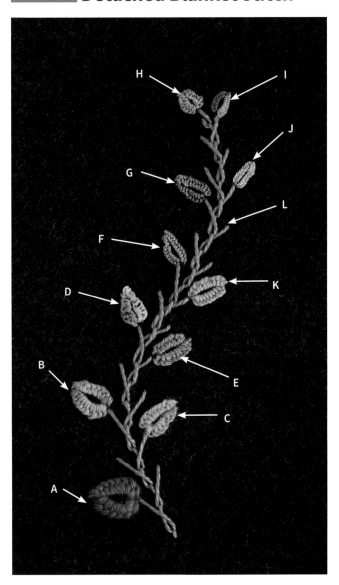

A   Detached blanket stitch (page 75) • *Tapestry wool*

B   Detached blanket stitch (page 75) • *Stranded cotton*

C   Detached blanket stitch (page 75) • *Crewel wool*

D   Detached blanket stitch (page 75) • *2mm silk ribbon*

E   Detached blanket stitch (page 75) • *Perle #8*

F   Detached blanket stitch (page 75) • *Perle #12*

G   Detached blanket stitch (page 75) • *EdMar Lola*

H   Detached blanket stitch (page 75) • *Perle #12*

I   Detached blanket stitch (page 75) • *Perle #12*

J   Detached blanket stitch (page 75) • *EdMar Frost*

K   Detached blanket stitch (page 75) • *Crochet cotton*

L   Twisted chain stitch (page 84) • *Perle #8*

Petals make up the part of the flower that attracts bees and other insects to pollinate the plant. They make the flower beautiful. I encourage you to choose glorious colors and interesting shapes to create your flowers. Also, make them bigger than you think they need to be.

PETALS AND FLOWERS

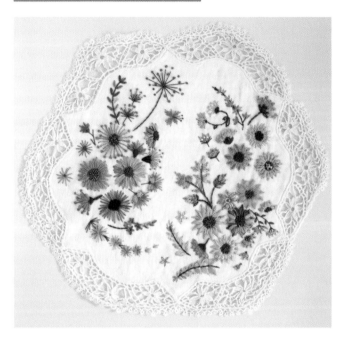

PETALS AND FLOWERS Straight Stitch *one*

A	*Center:* Colonial knot (page 74) • *Perle #8*
	Petals: Straight stitch (page 83) • *EdMar Frost*
B	*Petals:* Straight stitch (page 83) • *Crewel wool*
	Calyx: Straight stitch (page 83) • *Crewel wool*
	Stem: Straight stitch (page 83) • *Perle #8*
C	*Center:* Single bead stitch (page 82) • *Nymo thread, beads*
	Petals: Straight stitch (page 83) • *Tapestry wool*
D	*Center:* Colonial knot (page 74) • *Perle #8;* Single bead stitch (page 82) • *Nymo thread, beads*
	Petals: Straight stitch (page 83), Colonial knot (page 74) • *Crewel wool*

E	*Petals:* Straight stitch (page 83) • *DMC stranded*
	Stem: Stem stitch (page 83) • *Crewel wool*
F	*Petals:* Straight stitch (page 83) • *Crewel wool, perle #12;* Colonial knot (page 74) • *Crewel wool*
	Stem: Straight stitch (page 83) • *Perle #12*
G	*Center:* Colonial knot (page 74) • *Perle #8*
	Petals: Straight stitch (page 83) • *4mm silk ribbon*
H	*Petals:* Straight stitch (page 83) • *Crewel wool*
	Calyx: Straight stitch (page 83) • *Crewel wool*

I	*Petals:* Straight stitch (page 83) • *Perle #12;* Colonial knot (page 74) • *Perle #8*
	Stem: Stem stitch (page 83) • *Perle #8*
J	*Center:* Colonial knot (page 74) • *Perle #8*
	Petals: Straight stitch (page 83) • *4mm silk ribbon, perle #8*
K	*Petals:* Straight stitch (page 83) • *Crewel wool*
	Stamens: Straight stitch (page 83), Colonial knot (page 74) • *Perle #12*
L	*Petals:* Straight stitch (page 83) • *Crochet cotton, metallic thread;* Single bead stitch (page 82) • *Nymo thread, beads*
	Calyx: Straight stitch (page 83) • *Crewel wool*
M	*Petals:* Straight stitch (page 83) • *Crewel wool;* Ribbon stitch (page 81) • *7mm silk ribbon*
	Calyx: Colonial knot (page 74) • *Perle #8*
	Stem: Straight stitch (page 83) • *Perle #8*
N	*Center:* Colonial knot (page 74) • *Perle #8*
	Petals: Straight stitch (page 83) • *EdMar Lola*
O	*Petals:* Straight stitch (page 83) • *Tapestry wool;* Colonial knot (page 74) • *Perle #8*
	Calyx: Straight stitch (page 83) • *Tapestry wool*
	Stem: Straight stitch (page 83) • *Tapestry wool*
P	*Center:* Colonial knot (page 74) • *Perle #8*
	Petals: Straight stitch (page 83) • *Crewel wool*
Q	*Petals:* Straight stitch (page 83) • *Crewel wool*
	Stem and leaves: Straight stitch (page 83) • *Perle #8*
R	*Petals:* Straight stitch (page 83) • *Crewel wool*
	Stem: Stem stitch (page 83) • *Perle #8*

A
Petals: Detached twisted chain stitch (page 75)
• *2mm silk ribbon*

Calyx: Colonial knot (page 74) • *Crewel wool*

Stem: Couching (page 74) • *Crewel wool*

Leaves: Lazy daisy stitch (page 79) • *Crewel wool*

B
Petals: Lazy daisy stitch (page 79) • *Perle #8, crewel wool*; Single bead stitch (page 82) • *Nymo thread*

Calyx: Straight stitch (page 83) • *Perle #8*

Stem: Straight stitch (page 83) • *Perle #8*

C
Petals: Detached twisted chain stitch (page 75)
• *Crochet cotton*

Calyx: Colonial knot (page 74) • *Crewel wool*

Stem: Couching (page 74) • *Crewel wool*

D
Petals: Knotted lazy daisy stitch (page 79)
• *Crewel wool*

Calyx: Lazy daisy stitch (page 79) • *Crewel wool*

E
Petals: Lazy daisy stitch (page 79) • *Perle #8*

Stem: Backstitch (page 67) • *Perle #12*

F
Center: Colonial knot (page 74) • *Perle #8*

Petals: Lazy daisy stitch (page 79) • *Crewel wool*

G
Center: Colonial knot (page 74) • *Crewel wool*

Petals: Twisted lazy daisy stitch (page 84)
• *Crochet cotton*

H
Petals: Knotted lazy daisy stitch (page 79)
• *Crewel wool*

Calyx: Knotted lazy daisy stitch (page 79)
• *Crewel wool*

Stem: Stem stitch (page 83) • *Crewel wool*

I
Center: Backstitch (page 67), Colonial knot (page 74)
• *Crewel wool*

Petals: Twisted lazy daisy stitch (page 84)
• *2mm silk ribbon*

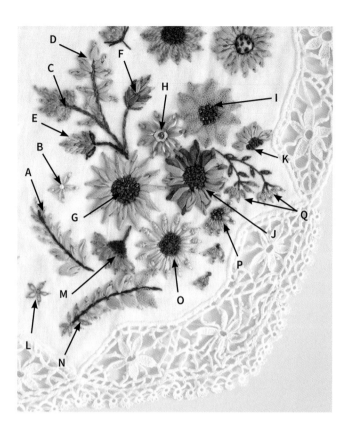

H	*Center:* Beaded/couched sequin (page 68) • *Nymo thread, beads*
	Petals: Lazy daisy stitch (page 79) • *Crewel wool*
I	*Center:* Single bead stitch (page 82) • *Nymo thread, beads*
	Petals: Lazy daisy stitch (page 79) • *Tulle thread*
J	*Center:* Colonial knot (page 74) • *Perle #8*
	Petals: Lazy daisy stitch (page 79) • *7mm silk ribbon*
K	*Center:* Colonial knot (page 74) • *Perle #8*
	Petals: Lazy daisy stitch (page 79) • *4mm silk ribbon*
L	*Center:* Colonial knot (page 74) • *Perle #12*
	Petals: Lazy daisy stitch (page 79) • *Perle #12*
M	*Petals:* Lazy daisy stitch (page 79) • *Crewel wool*
	Calyx: Straight stitch (page 83) • *Crewel wool*
	Stem: Straight stitch (page 83) • *Crewel wool*
N	*Petals:* Lazy daisy stitch (page 79) • *Assorted threads, silk ribbons*
	Stem: Thin stem stitch (page 83) • *Perle #12*
O	*Center:* Colonial knot (page 74) • *Perle #8*
	Petals: Bullion lazy daisy stitch (page 72) • *Crochet cotton*
P	*Center:* Single bead stitch (page 82) • *Nymo thread*
	Petals: Lazy daisy stitch with bead (page 79) • *Perle #8*
Q	*Petals:* Lazy daisy stitch (page 79) • *Perle #12*
	Stem: Couching (page 74) • *Perle #12*
	Leaves: Lazy daisy stitch (page 79) • *Perle #12*

A	*Petals:* Twisted lazy daisy stitch (page 84) • *Assorted threads, silk ribbons*
	Stem: Stem stitch (page 83) • *Crewel wool*
B	*Center:* Single bead stitch (page 82) • *Nymo thread, beads*
	Petals: Lazy daisy stitch (page 79) • *Crochet cotton*
C	*Petals:* Knotted lazy daisy stitch (page 79) • *Crewel wool*
	Stem: Thin stem stitch (page 83) • *Perle #8*
D	*Petals:* Knotted lazy daisy stitch (page 79) • *4mm silk ribbon*
	Stem: Stem stitch (page 83) • *Perle #8*
E	*Petals:* Lazy daisy stitch (page 79) • *Stranded cotton*
	Calyx: Lazy daisy stitch (page 79) • *Crewel wool*
	Stem: Stem stitch (page 83) • *Crewel wool*
F	*Petals:* Lazy daisy stitch (page 79) • *2mm silk ribbon*
	Calyx: Straight stitch (page 83) • *Perle #8*
	Stem: Stem stitch (page 83) • *Perle #8*
G	*Center:* Single bead stitch (page 82) • *Nymo thread, beads*; Colonial knot (page 74) • *Perle #12*
	Petals: Bullion lazy daisy stitch (page 72) • *4mm silk ribbon*

ROSE PETALS *one*

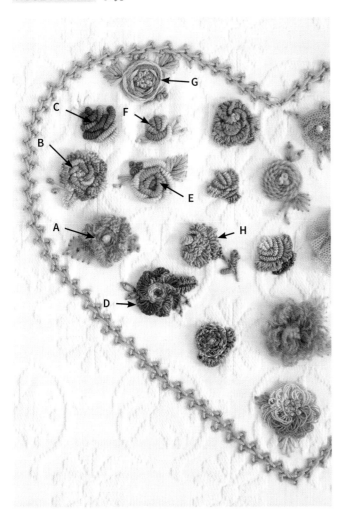

A	Bullion rose technique (page 72) *Center:* Colonial knot (page 74) • *Crewel wool* *Petals:* Spiderweb rose (page 82), Cast-on stitch (page 73) with 2 needles • *Crewel wool* *Leaves:* Fishbone stitch (page 77), Colonial knot (page 74) • *Crewel wool*
B	Bullion rose technique (page 72) *Center:* Colonial knot (page 74), Bullion knot (page 72) • *Perle #8* *Petals:* Cast-on stitch (page 73) • *Perle #8* *Leaves:* Detached blanket stitch (page 75), Straight stitch (page 83), Colonial knot (page 74) • *Perle #8*
C	Upright rose technique (page 85) *Calyx:* Bullion knot (page 72) • *Stranded cotton* *Petals:* Bullion knot (page 72) • *Stranded cotton* *Stamens:* Straight stitch (page 83) • *Stranded cotton*
D	Bullion rose technique (page 72) *Center:* Spiderweb rose (page 82), Colonial knot (page 74) • *Perle #8* *Petals:* Cast-on stitch (page 73) with 2 needles • *Perle #8* *Leaves:* Detached blanket stitch (page 75), Lazy daisy stitch (page 79) • *Perle #8*
E	Bullion rose technique (page 72) *Center:* Bullion knot (page 72) • *Stranded cotton* *Petals:* Bullion knot (page 72) • *Stranded cotton* *Leaves:* Fishbone stitch (page 77), Lazy daisy stitch (page 79) • *Stranded cotton* *Buds:* Colonial knot (page 74) • *Stranded cotton*
F	Upright rose technique (page 85) *Petals:* Bullion knot (page 72) • *Stranded cotton* *Leaves:* Lazy daisy stitch (page 79) • *Stranded cotton*
G	Spiderweb rose (page 82) *Center:* Colonial knot (page 74) • *Perle #8* *Petals:* Spiderweb rose variation (page 82) • *Stranded cotton* *Leaves:* Fishbone stitch (page 77) • *Stranded cotton* *Buds:* Colonial knot (page 74) • *Stranded cotton*
H	Upright rose technique (page 85) *Center:* Looped cast-on stitch (page 80) • *Perle #8* *Petals:* Cast-on stitch (page 73) with 1 and 2 needles • *Perle #8* *Stem:* Stem stitch (page 83) • *Perle #8* *Leaves:* Detached blanket stitch (page 75) • *Perle #8*

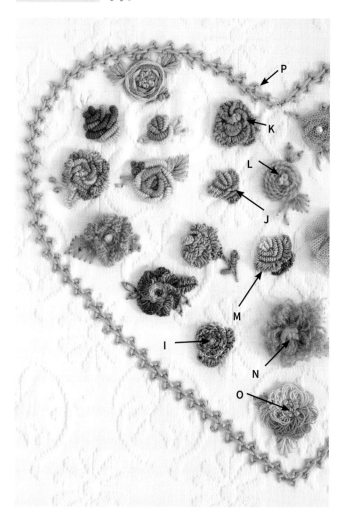

I	Spiderweb rose (page 82)
	Center: Bullion knot (page 72) • *EdMar Lola*
	Petals: Spiderweb rose (page 82) • *EdMar Bouclé*
	Leaves: Cast-on stitch (page 73) • *EdMar Frost*
J	Upright rose technique (page 85)
	Center: Bullion knot (page 72) • *Perle #8*
	Petals: Cast-on stitch (page 73) • *Perle #8*
	Calyx: Bullion knot (page 72), Cast-on stitch (page 73) • *Perle #8*
K	Bullion rose technique (page 72)
	Center: Looped bullion knot stitch (page 80) • *Crochet cotton*
	Petals: Cast-on stitch (page 73) • *Crochet cotton*
	Leaves: Cast-on stitch (page 73) • *Crochet cotton*
L	Spiderweb rose (page 82)
	Center: Colonial knot (page 74) • *Crewel wool*
	Petals: Spiderweb rose (page 82) • *Crewel wool*
	Leaves: Lazy daisy stitch (page 79), Fishbone stitch (page 77) • *Crewel wool*
	Twigs: Straight stitch (page 83) • *Crewel wool*
	Bud: Colonial knot (page 74) • *Crewel wool*
M	Upright rose technique (page 85)
	Petals: Bullion knot (page 72), Cast-on stitch (page 73) • *EdMar Lola*
	Calyx: Cast-on stitch (page 73) • *EdMar Lola*
N	*Center:* Colonial knot (page 74) • *Crewel wool*
	Petals: Ghiordes knot stitch (page 78), untrimmed • *Crewel wool*
	Leaves: Fishbone stitch (page 77) • *Crewel wool*
O	*Center:* Colonial knot (page 74) • *Perle #8*
	Petals: Ghiordes knot stitch (page 78), untrimmed • *Stranded cotton*
	Leaves: Fishbone stitch (page 77) • *Stranded cotton*
P	Spanish knotted feather stitch (page 82) • *Crochet cotton*

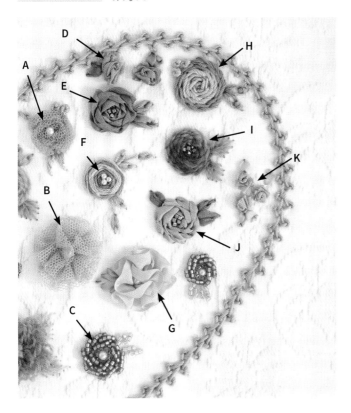

A
Center: Single bead stitch (page 82) • *Nymo thread, bead*

Petals: Spiderweb rose (page 82) • *Tulle thread*

Leaves: Twisted lazy daisy stitch (page 84) • *Crochet cotton*

Buds: Colonial knot (page 74) • *Crochet cotton*

B
Free-form flower with beaded center (page 78) • *Tulle thread, Nymo thread, bead*

C
Center: Single bead stitch (page 82) • *Nymo thread, bead*

Petals: Beaded rose (page 70) • *Nymo thread, beads*

Leaves: Beaded leaf (page 69) • *Nymo thread, beads*

D
Petals: Ruched rose (page 81) • *7mm silk thread*

Leaves: Ribbon stitch (page 81) • *4mm silk ribbon*

E
Center: Single bead stitch (page 82) • *Nymo thread, beads*

Petals: Spiderweb rose (page 82) • *7mm silk ribbon*

Leaves: Lazy daisy stitch (page 79) • *4mm silk ribbon*

F
Center: Single bead stitch (page 82) • *Nymo thread, beads*

Petals: Spiderweb rose (page 82) • *Stranded cotton*

Leaves: Lazy daisy stitch (page 79), Straight stitch (page 83) • *Crochet cotton*

G
Center: Free-form flower with beaded center (page 78) • *13mm silk ribbon*

Leaves: Fishbone stitch (page 77) • *4mm silk ribbon*

H
Center: Colonial knot (page 74) • *Perle #8*

Petals: Stem stitch rose (page 83) • *Crochet cotton*

Leaves: Bullion lazy daisy stitch (page 72), Colonial knot (page 74) • *Crochet cotton*

Buds: Colonial knot (page 74) • *Crochet cotton*

I
Center: Single bead stitch (page 82) • *Nymo thread, beads*

Petals: Stem stitch rose (page 83) • *Crewel wool*

Leaves: Fishbone stitch (page 77) • *Crewel wool*

J
Center: Single bead stitch (page 82) • *Nymo thread, bead*

Petals: Stem stitch rose (page 83) • *4mm silk ribbon*

Leaves: Lazy daisy stitch (page 79) • *4mm silk ribbon*

K
Center: Ruched rose (page 81) • *4mm silk ribbon*

Leaves: Ribbon stitch (page 81) • *4mm silk ribbon*

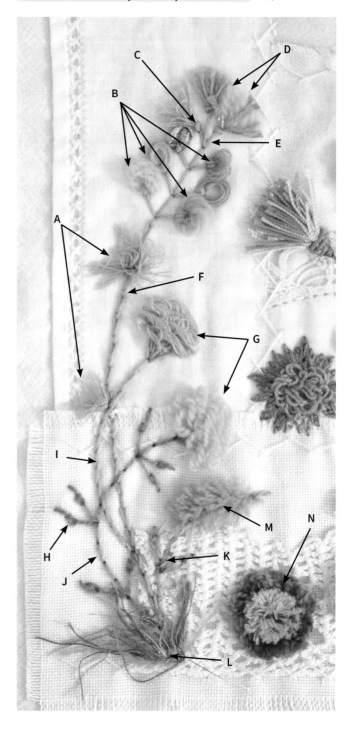

A	Tufting (page 84) • *Stranded cotton*
B	Detached loop stitch (page 75) • *Crewel wool, stranded cotton, crochet cotton, metallic thread*
C	Grab stitch (page 79) • *Crochet cotton*
D	Tufting (page 84) • *Crewel wool, stranded cotton, perle #8, metallic thread*
E	Straight stitch (page 83) • *Crochet cotton*
F	Uneven chain stitch (page 85) • *Crochet cotton*
G	Ghiordes knot stitch (page 78), untrimmed • *Stranded cotton, crewel wool*
H	Twisted chain stitch (page 84) • *Crewel wool*
I	Stem stitch (page 83) • *Crochet cotton*
J	Backstitch (page 67) • *Crewel wool*
K	Couching (page 74) • *Crewel wool*
L	Tufting (page 84) • *Crewel wool, stranded cotton, metallic thread (1 needle)*
M	Ghiordes knot stitch (page 78), trimmed • *Crewel wool*
N	*Center:* Ghiordes knot stitch (page 78), trimmed • *Stranded cotton* *Petals:* Ghiordes knot stitch (page 78), untrimmed • *Crewel wool*

F   *Petals:* Tufting (page 84) • *Stranded cotton*

     Calyx: Couching (page 74) • *Perle #8*

G   *Stem:* Backstitch (page 67), Whipping stitch (page 86) • *Crochet cotton*

     Leaves: Straight stitch (page 83) • *Crochet cotton*

     Center: Colonial knot (page 74) • *Perle #8*

H   *Petals:* Ghiordes knot stitch (page 78), trimmed • *Crewel wool, stranded cotton*

     Stem: Palestrina knot stitch (page 80) • *Perle #8*

I   *Flower:* Ghiordes knot stitch (page 78), trimmed • *Crewel wool, stranded cotton, metallic thread*

     Center: Ghiordes knot stitch (page 78), untrimmed • *Perle #8*

J   *Petals:* Lazy daisy stitch (page 79) • *Perle #8*

     Stem: Twisted chain stitch (page 84) • *Perle #8*

K   *Petals:* Ghiordes knot stitch (page 78), untrimmed • *2mm silk ribbon*

     Calyx: Straight stitch (page 83) • *Crochet cotton*

     Stem: Straight stitch (page 83) • *Crochet cotton*

     Leaves: Lazy daisy stitch (page 79) • *Crochet cotton*

L   *Center:* Colonial knot (page 74) • *Perle #8*

     Petals: Ghiordes knot stitch (page 78), untrimmed • *Crewel wool*

M   *Flower:* Ghiordes knot stitch (page 78) • *Crewel wool*

N   *Petals:* Ghiordes knot stitch (page 78), untrimmed • *EdMar Lola*

     Calyx: Straight stitch (page 83) • *Crochet cotton*

     Stem: Straight stitch (page 83) • *Crochet cotton*

     Leaves: Lazy daisy stitch (page 79) • *Crochet cotton*

O   *Stem:* Fern stitch (page 77) • *Crewel wool*

P   *Flower:* Ghiordes knot stitch (page 78) • *Crewel wool*

     Stem: Stem stitch (page 83) • *Crewel wool*

A   *Flower:* Tufting (page 84) • *EdMar Lola*

     Calyx: Detached blanket stitch (page 75) • *Perle #8*

     Stem: Portuguese knotted stem stitch (page 80) • *EdMar Frost*

B   *Petals:* Ghiordes knot stitch (page 78), untrimmed • *Stranded cotton*

     Calyx: Straight stitch (page 83) • *Crochet cotton*

     Stem: Straight stitch (page 83) • *Crochet cotton*

     Leaves: Lazy daisy stitch (page 79) • *Crochet cotton*

C   *Petals:* Ghiordes knot stitch (page 78), trimmed • *Tapestry yarn*

     Calyx: Straight stitch (page 83) • *Crewel wool*

D   *Stem:* Stem stitch (page 83) • *Crewel wool*

E   *Petals:* Ghiordes knot stitch (page 78), trimmed • *Crewel wool*

     Calyx: Straight stitch (page 83) • *Crewel wool*

COLONIAL AND FRENCH KNOT FLOWERS

The humble colonial and French knots make up a plethora of flower heads.

A	*Petals:* Colonial knot (page 74) • *Perle #8;* Ribbon stitch (page 81) • *4mm silk ribbon*
	Stem: Grab stitch (page 79) • *Crewel wool*
	Leaves: Straight stitch (page 83) • *Crewel wool*
B	*Petals:* Straight stitch (page 83), Colonial knot (page 74), French knot (page 78) • *2mm silk ribbon, crewel wool, perle #8*
	Stem: Stem stitch (page 83) • *Perle #8*
	Leaves: Fly stitch (page 78) • *Crewel wool, 2mm silk ribbon*
C	*Petals:* French knot (page 78), loose • *Crewel wool, 2mm silk ribbon, stranded cotton*
	Calyx: Straight stitch (page 83) • *Perle #8*
D	*Center:* Colonial knot (page 74) • *Perle #12*
	Petals: Colonial knot (page 74) • *2mm silk ribbon, crewel wool*
	Stem: Straight stitch (page 83) • *Perle #8*
	Leaves: Lazy daisy stitch (page 79), Twisted lazy daisy stitch (page 84) • *Perle #8*
E	*Petals:* Colonial knot (page 74), French knot (page 78) • *4mm silk ribbon, Nymo thread, beads*
	Leaves: Ribbon stitch (page 81) • *7mm silk ribbon*
F	*Buds:* French knot (page 78) • *Perle #12*
	Stem: Feather stitch (page 76) • *Perle #12*
G	*Stem:* Couching (page 74) • *Crewel wool*
	Leaves: Ribbon stitch (page 81) • *7mm silk ribbon*
H	*Center:* Colonial knot (page 74) • *Perle #8*
	Petals: Colonial knot (page 74) • *Perle #8, crewel wool, 2mm silk ribbon*
	Stem: Straight stitch (page 83) • *Perle #8*
I	*Petals:* Colonial knot (page 74) • *Perle #8, crewel wool, 2mm silk ribbon*
	Stem: Stem stitch (page 83) • *Perle #8*
	Leaves: Lazy daisy stitch (page 79) • *2mm silk ribbon*
	Long leaves: Straight stitch (page 83) • *2mm silk ribbon*
	Twigs: Straight stitch (page 83), French knot (page 78) • *Perle #8*
J	*Petals:* Colonial knot (page 74), French knot (page 78) • *Tapestry wool, 2mm silk ribbon, needlepoint ribbon;* Ghiordes knot stitch (page 78), Straight stitch (page 83) • *Crewel wool*
	Stem: Stem stitch (page 83) • *Crewel wool*
	Leaves: Straight stitch (page 83) • *4mm silk ribbon*
K	*Petals:* Colonial knot (page 74) • *7mm silk ribbon, crewel wool, perle #8, crochet cotton*
	Stem: Backstitch (page 67), Whipping stitch (page 86) • *Crochet cotton*
	Leaves: Fishbone stitch: open (page 77); Fly stitch (page 78), Twisted lazy daisy stitch (page 84) • *Crochet cotton*

A	*Center:* Beaded/couched sequin (page 68) • *Nymo thread, sequin, bead*	
	Petals: Blanket stitch (page 71) • *Perle #8, crewel wool*	
	Stem: Straight stitch (page 83) • *Perle #8*	
	Leaves: Bullion lazy daisy stitch (page 72) • *Crewel wool*	

B

Center: Colonial knot (page 74) • *Crewel wool*

Petals: Blanket stitch (page 71) • *Perle #8*

Stem: Uneven chain stitch (page 85) • *Perle #8*

Leaves: Blanket stitch (page 71) • *Crewel wool*

C

Petals: Blanket stitch (page 71), Detached blanket stitch (page 75) • *2mm silk ribbon, crewel wool*

Calyx: Detached blanket stitch (page 75) • *Perle #8*

Stem: Feather twig stitch (page 76) • *Crewel wool*

D

Petals: Blanket stitch (page 71) • *Perle #8, perle #12, stranded cotton, 2mm silk ribbon;* Colonial knot (page 74) • *Crewel wool*

Stem: Thin stem stitch (page 83) • *Crewel wool*

Leaves: Blanket stitch (page 71) • *Crewel wool*

E

Center: Colonial knot (page 74) • *Crewel wool*

Petals: Blanket stitch (page 71) • *Crewel wool*

Stem: Stem stitch (page 83) • *Perle #8*

Leaves: Fishbone stitch (page 77) • *Perle #8*

F

Petals: Blanket stitch (page 71) • *Perle #8, perle #12, crochet cotton, 2mm silk ribbon, crewel wool*

Calyx: Straight stitch (page 83), Colonial knot (page 74) • *Perle #8*

Stem: Twisted chain stitch (page 84) • *Perle #8*

Leaves: Ribbon stitch (page 81) • *7mm silk ribbon*

G

Petals: Blanket stitch (page 71), Lazy daisy stitch (page 79) • *Crewel wool*

Stem: Uneven chain stitch (page 85) • *Crewel wool*

Leaves: Blanket stitch (page 71) • *Crewel wool*

H

Petals: Blanket stitch (page 71), Lazy daisy stitch (page 79) • *2mm silk ribbon*

Stem: Uneven chain stitch (page 85) • *Crewel wool*

Leaves: Blanket stitch (page 71) • *Crochet cotton*

I

Petals: Blanket stitch (page 71), Detached blanket stitch (page 75) • *Perle #8, perle #12, 2mm silk ribbon, crewel wool*

Stem: Thin stem stitch (page 83) • *Perle #8*

Leaves: Blanket stitch (page 71) • *Perle #8*

J

Petals: Blanket stitch (page 71) • *Perle #8*

Calyx: Detached blanket stitch (page 75) • *Perle #8*

Stem: Thin stem stitch (page 83) • *Perle #8*

Leaves: Straight stitch (page 83) • *Perle #8*

Stamen: Straight stitch (page 83) • *Perle #8;* Single bead stitch (page 82) • *Nymo thread, bead*

K

Center: Single bead stitch (page 82) • *Nymo thread, bead*

Petals: Blanket stitch (page 71) • *Perle #8, 2mm silk ribbon, crewel wool*

Calyx: Blanket stitch (page 71) • *Crewel wool*

Stem: Stem stitch (page 83) • *Crewel wool*

Leaves: Twisted lazy daisy stitch (page 84) • *Crewel wool*

L

Center: Colonial knot (page 74) • *Perle #8*

Petals: Blanket stitch (page 71) • *Perle #8, crewel wool*

Calyx: Blanket stitch (page 71) • *Perle #8*

Stem: Uneven chain stitch (page 85) • *Perle #8*

Buds: Colonial knot (page 74), Blanket stitch (page 71) • *Perle #8*

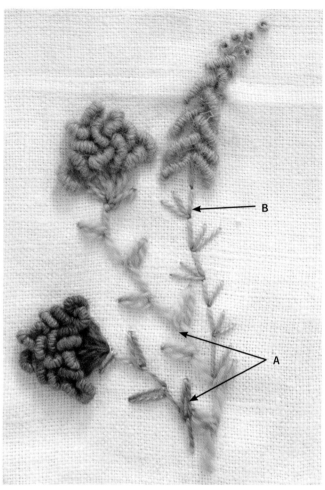

A
Petals: Looped bullion knot stitch (page 80) • *Crewel wool, perle #8*

Calyx: Straight stitch (page 83) • *Crewel wool*

Stem: Chain feathered stitch (page 73) • *Crewel wool, perle #8*

B
Petals: Bullion knot (page 72), Colonial knot (page 74) • *Crewel wool*

Stem: Straight stitch (page 83) • *Perle #8*

Leaves: Straight stitch (page 83) • *Perle #8*

A	*Center:* Single bead stitch (page 82) • *Nymo thread, bead*
	Petals: Looped bullion knot stitch (page 80) • *Crewel wool, perle #8*
	Petals: Looped bullion knot stitch (page 80), Straight stitch (page 83) • *Crewel wool, stranded cotton, EdMar Lola*
B	*Stem:* Rope stitch (page 81) • *Perle #8*
	Leaves: Straight stitch (page 83) • *Perle #8*
C	*Petals:* Bullion knot (page 72) • *Twisted silk, crewel wool, EdMar Lola, perle #8*
	Calyx: Straight stitch (page 83) • *Crewel wool*
	Stem: Twisted chain stitch (page 84) • *Crewel wool*
	Leaves: Beaded leaf (page 69) • *Nymo thread, beads*
	Stamen: French knot (page 78) • *Crewel wool*; Single bead stitch (page 82) • *Nymo thread, beads*
D	*Petals:* Looped bullion knot stitch (page 80) • *Stranded cotton, crewel wool, crochet cotton*
	Calyx: Bullion knot (page 72) • *Perle #8*
	Stem: Stem stitch (page 83) • *Perle #8, crewel wool*
	Leaves: Fly stitch (page 78), Straight stitch (page 83) • *Perle #8*
	Stamens: Straight stitch (page 83) • *Stranded cotton*
E	*Petals:* Bullion knot (page 72) • *Perle #12*
	Stamens: Straight stitch (page 83), Colonial knot (page 74) • *Perle #12*

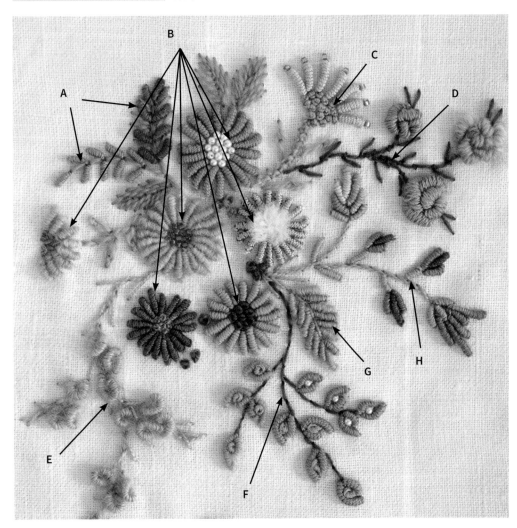

A	***Petals:*** Bullion knot (page 72) • *Perle #8*
	Stem: Straight stitch (page 83) • *Crewel wool*
	Leaves: Fishbone stitch (page 77) • *Crewel wool*
B	***Center:*** Tufting (page 84) • *Crewel wool*; Colonial knot (page 74) • *Perle #8*; Single bead stitch (page 82) • *Nymo thread, beads*
	Petals: Bullion knot (page 72) • *EdMar Lola, crochet cotton, perle #8, stranded cotton*
	Leaves: Fishbone stitch (page 77) • *Crewel wool*
C	***Petals:*** Bullion knot (page 72) • *Crochet cotton*; Single bead stitch (page 82) • *Nymo thread, beads*
	Calyx: Colonial knot (page 74) • *Stranded cotton*
	Stem: Palestrina knot stitch (page 80) • *Crewel wool*
	Leaves: Twisted lazy daisy stitch (page 84) • *Crewel wool*
D	***Petals:*** Bullion knot (page 72) with 2 needles • *Crewel wool, stranded cotton, perle #8*
	Stem: Couching (page 74) • *Crewel wool*
	Leaves: Straight stitch (page 83) • *Crewel wool*

E	***Petals:*** Looped bullion knot stitch (page 80) • *Crewel wool*
	Stem: Twisted chain stitch (page 84) • *Perle #8*
F	***Center:*** Colonial knot (page 74) • *Crochet cotton*; Single bead stitch (page 82) • *Nymo thread, bead*
	Petals: Bullion knot (page 72) • *Crewel wool, perle #8*
	Stem: Straight stitch (page 83) • *Perle #8*
G	***Petals:*** Bullion knot (page 72) • *Crewel wool, perle #8*
	Stem: Straight stitch (page 83) • *Perle #8*
H	***Petals:*** Bullion knot (page 72) • *Stranded cotton, perle #8*
	Calyx: Bullion knot (page 72) • *Perle #8*
	Stem: Stem stitch (page 83) • *Perle #8*
	Leaves: Bullion knot (page 72) • *Perle #8*

CAST-ON STITCH FLOWERS

CAST-ON STITCH FLOWERS *one*

A	***Petals:*** Cast-on stitch (page 73) • *Crewel wool, EdMar Lola*
	Calyx: Cast-on stitch (page 73) • *Crewel wool, EdMar Lola*
	Stem: Straight stitch (page 83) • *Crewel wool, EdMar Lola*
	Leaves: Lazy daisy stitch (page 79) • *Crewel wool, EdMar Lola*
B	***Petals:*** Cast-on stitch (page 73) • *Crewel wool, EdMar Lola*
	Stem: Stem stitch (page 83) • *Perle #8*
	Twigs: Fern stitch (page 77), Colonial knot (page 74) • *Perle #8*
C	***Center:*** Tufting (page 84) • *Crewel wool*; Single bead stitch (page 82) • *Nymo thread, beads*; Colonial knot (page 74) • *Crochet cotton*
	Petals: Cast-on stitch (page 73) • *Crochet cotton, crewel wool, stranded cotton, perle #8*
	Leaves: Cast-on stitch (page 73) • *Perle #8*; Fly stitch (page 78) • *4mm silk ribbon*
	Twigs: Fern stitch (page 77), Colonial knot (page 74) • *Perle #8*
D	***Petals:*** Cast-on stitch (page 73) • *Crochet cotton, perle #8*
	Calyx: Cast-on stitch (page 73) • *Perle #8*
	Stem: Stem stitch (page 83) • *Perle #8*
	Leaves: Bullion lazy daisy stitch (page 72) • *Perle #8*
	Stamens: Straight stitch (page 83) • *Perle #8*; Single bead stitch (page 82) • *Nymo thread, beads*
E	***Center:*** Colonial knot (page 74) • *Perle #8*
	Petals: Looped cast-on stitch (page 80) • *EdMar Lola, stranded cotton, perle #8*
	Leaves: Lazy daisy stitch (page 79) • *Perle #8*

	Petals: Looped cast-on stitch (page 80) • *EdMar Lola, crewel wool*
A	*Stem:* Straight stitch (page 83) • *Perle #8*
	Leaves: Straight stitch (page 83) • *Perle #8*
	Petals: Looped cast-on stitch (page 80) • *EdMar Lola, perle #12*
B	*Stem:* Stem stitch (page 83) • *Perle #8*
	Leaves: Fishbone stitch (page 77) • *Perle #8*
	Center: Colonial knot (page 74) • *Perle #8*
C	*Petals:* Looped cast-on stitch (page 80) • *Perle #8, perle #12*
	Stem: Feather twig stitch (page 76) • *Crewel wool*

A

Petals: Looped cast-on stitch (page 80) • *Crewel wool, perle #8, perle #12*

Calyx: Straight stitch (page 83) • *Perle #8*; Looped cast-on stitch (page 80) • *Perle #12*

Stem: Palestrina knot stitch (page 80) • *Perle #8*

Twigs: Straight stitch (page 83) • *Perle #12*

Stamens: Straight stitch (page 83), Colonial knot (page 74) • *Perle #12*

B

Center: Colonial knot (page 74) • *Perle #12*; Single bead stitch (page 82) • *Nymo thread, beads*; Tufting (page 84) • *Perle #8*

Petals: Looped cast-on stitch (page 80) • *Stranded cotton, perle #8, crewel wool*

Leaves: Bullion lazy daisy stitch (page 72) • *Crewel wool*

C

Petals: Cast-on stitch (page 73) with 2 needles • *Stranded cotton, crewel wool*

Calyx: Straight stitch (page 83) • *Stranded cotton, crewel wool*

Stem: Stem stitch (page 83) • *Crewel wool*

Leaves: Stem stitch (page 83) • *Crewel wool, stranded cotton*

LET'S MIX IT UP Petals and Flowers

It is so much fun to create your own fantasy flowers by combining stitches and working with different types of thread. I have created a few to get your creative juices flowing! To highlight the flower heads, I have used only stem stitch for the stems and lazy daisy stitch for the leaves.

A
Calyx: Straight stitch (page 83) • *4mm silk ribbon, stranded cotton*

Petals: Straight stitch (page 83) • *Tulle thread*

Stamens: Single bead stitch (page 82) • *Nymo thread, beads*

B
Calyx: Woven spiderweb (page 87) • *Stranded cotton*; Colonial knot (page 74) • *Perle #8*

Petals: Tufting (page 84) • *Crewel wool*

C
Calyx: Straight stitch (page 83) • *Perle #8*

Petals: Bullion lazy daisy stitch (page 72) • *Perle #8*

Stamens: Straight stitch (page 83) • *Crewel wool*; Single bead stitch (page 82) • *Nymo thread, beads*

D
Calyx: Cast-on stitch (page 73) • *Perle #8*

Petals: Free-form flower with beaded center (page 78) • *14mm silk ribbon*

Stamens: Twisted lazy daisy stitch (page 84) • *Perle #8*

E
Calyx: Cast-on stitch (page 73) • *Crewel wool*

Petals: Woven picot (page 86) • *Perle #8*; Ribbon stitch (page 81) • *4mm silk ribbon*

Stamens: Straight stitch (page 83), French knot (page 78) • *Perle #12*

F
Calyx: Ribbon stitch (page 81) • *7mm silk ribbon*

Petals: Ribbon stitch (page 81) • *7mm silk ribbon*

Stamens: Twisted lazy daisy stitch (page 84), Straight stitch (page 83), Colonial knot (page 74) • *Crewel wool*

G
Calyx: Bullion knot (page 72), Cast-on stitch (page 73) • *Crewel wool*

Petals: Cast-on stitch (page 73) • *Perle #8 (2 needles)*

Stamens: Straight stitch (page 83) • *Crewel wool*; Single bead stitch (page 82) • *Nymo thread, beads*

H
Petals: Bullion knot (page 72) • *Crochet cotton*; Bullion lazy daisy stitch (page 72) • *Perle #8*

Stamens: Colonial knot (page 74) • *Perle #8*

I
Petals: Bullion knot (page 72) • *Stranded cotton*; Straight stitch (page 83) • *4mm silk ribbon*; Beaded backstitch (page 67), Single bead stitch (page 82) • *Nymo thread, beads*; Tufting (page 84) • *Crewel wool*

J
Calyx: Bullion knot (page 72) • *Stranded cotton*

Petals: Straight stitch (page 83) • *7mm silk ribbon*

Stamens: Straight stitch (page 83), Colonial knot (page 74) • *Perle #12*

K
Petals: Straight stitch (page 83) • *2mm silk ribbon, crewel wool*

Center: Colonial knot (page 74) • *Perle #8*; Tufting (page 84) • *Crewel wool*

L
Petals: Lazy daisy stitch (page 79) • *4mm silk ribbon*

Center: Looped cast-on stitch (page 80) • *Perle #8*

Stamens: Straight stitch (page 83), French knot (page 78) • *Perle #8*

The centers of the flowers are vital to the overall appearance of the embroidery. Make them large enough to accommodate the many petals that will surround them. To showcase the centers, I have used the same stitch (lazy daisy) in different threads; however, when creating your flowers any stitch may be used for the petals.

EMBROIDERY STITCHES FOR FLOWER CENTERS

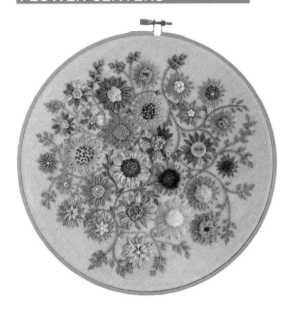

A	Beaded/couched sequin (page 68) • *Nymo thread, bead, sequin*
B	Beaded/couched sequin (page 68) • *Nymo thread, bead, sequin*
C	Bullion rose technique (page 72), Bullion knot (page 72) • *Perle #8*
D	Straight stitch (page 83) • *Crewel wool*
E	Ruched rose (page 81) • *7mm silk ribbon*
F	Ruched rose (page 81) • *4mm silk ribbon*
G	Colonial knot (page 74) • *Crewel wool*
H	Bullion rose technique (page 72), Cast-on stitch (page 73), Colonial knot (page 74) • *Crewel wool*
I	Colonial knot (page 74) • *Perle #8*; Single bead stitch (page 82) • *Nymo thread, beads*
J	Beaded/couched sequin (page 68) • *Nymo thread, sequin, beads*
K	Woven spiderweb (page 87) • *EdMar Lola*
L	Spiderweb rose (page 82) • *Crochet cotton*; Beaded/couched sequin (page 68) • *Nymo thread, bead, sequin*
M	Single bead stitch (page 82) • *Nymo thread, beads*; Colonial knot (page 74) • *Perle #8*

EMBROIDERY STITCHES FOR FLOWER CENTERS *one*

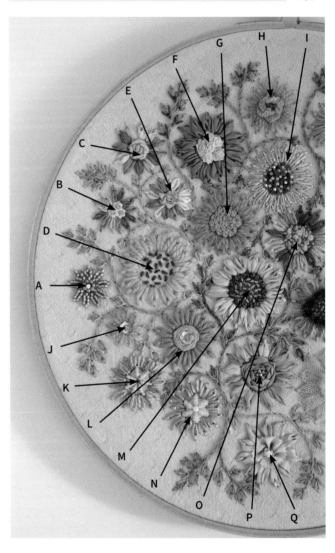

N	Woven spiderweb (page 87) • *Crewel wool*; Single bead stitch (page 82) • *Nymo thread, beads*
O	Colonial knot (page 74) • *Crewel wool, stranded cotton*; Single bead stitch (page 82) • *Nymo thread, beads*
P	Spiderweb rose (page 82) • *7mm silk ribbon*; Single bead stitch (page 82) • *Nymo thread, beads*
Q	Free-form flower with beaded center (page 78) • *Ribbon, bead*

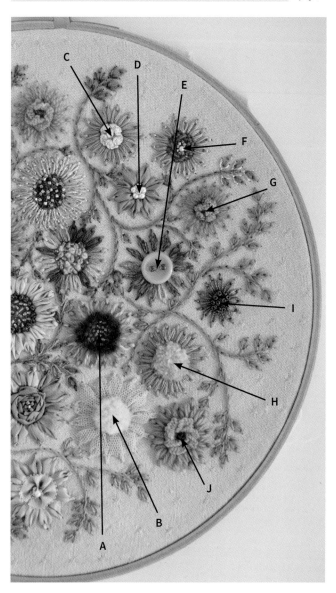

A Single bead stitch (page 82) • *Nymo thread, beads*; Ghiordes knot stitch (page 78), trimmed • *Crewel wool*

B Ghiordes knot stitch (page 78), trimmed • *Crewel wool*

C Drizzle stitch (page 76) • *EdMar Lola*

D Beaded forget-me-knot (page 69) • *Nymo thread, beads*

E Buttons and beads • *Nymo thread, beads*

F Beaded rose (page 70) • *Nymo thread, beads*

G Drizzle stitch (page 76) • *Perle #8*

H Ghiordes knot stitch (page 78), trimmed • *Crewel wool, stranded cotton*

I Beaded tassel (page 71) • *Nymo thread, beads*

J Bullion rose technique (page 72), Colonial knot (page 74), Cast-on stitch (page 73) • *Crewel wool*

EMBROIDERY STITCHES FOR CALYXES

Calyxes hold the petals in place. When viewing a flower from the side we see them doing their work.

A	*Calyx:* Cast-on stitch (page 73), Bullion knot (page 72) • *Crewel wool*
	Petals: Straight stitch (page 83) • *Crewel wool*
B	*Calyx:* Ribbon stitch (page 81) • *4mm silk ribbon*
	Petals: Straight stitch (page 83) • *Perle #8, crewel wool*
C	*Calyx:* Woven spiderweb (page 87), Colonial knot (page 74) • *Stranded cotton*
	Petals: Straight stitch (page 83) • *2mm silk ribbon*
D	*Calyx:* Lazy daisy stitch (page 79), Colonial knot (page 74) • *4mm silk ribbon*
	Petals: Straight stitch (page 83) • *Crewel wool*
E	*Calyx:* Bullion knot (page 72) • *Crochet cotton*
	Petals: Straight stitch (page 83) • *Crochet cotton*
F	*Calyx:* Straight stitch (page 83), Colonial knot (page 74) • *Crewel wool*
	Petals: Straight stitch (page 83), Colonial knot (page 74) • *Crewel wool*
G	*Calyx:* Colonial knot (page 74) • *Stranded cotton*
	Petals: Straight stitch (page 83) • *Crewel wool*
H	*Calyx:* Straight stitch (page 83) • *Crewel wool*
	Petals: Straight stitch (page 83) • *Crewel wool, Very Velvet (by Rainbow Gallery) thread*
I	*Calyx:* Cast-on stitch (page 73), Bullion knot (page 72) • *Crochet cotton*
	Petals: Straight stitch (page 83) • *Tulle thread*

EMBROIDERY STITCHES FOR FLOWER BUDS

Buds, the sweetness of them! The buds should not overpower the main flowers in the design. Keep your buds busy and delightful. To showcase the buds, I have used the same stitch (lazy daisy) for the leaves and stem stitch for the stems throughout; however, when creating your buds any stitch may be used.

EMBROIDERY STITCHES FOR FLOWER BUDS *one*

A	*Calyx:* Straight stitch (page 83) • *Crochet cotton*
	Bud: Straight stitch (page 83) • *Perle #8*
B	*Calyx:* Cast-on stitch (page 73), Bullion knot (page 72) • *Perle #8*
	Bud: Woven picot (page 86), Drizzle stitch (page 76) • *Perle #8*
C	*Calyx:* Cast-on stitch (page 73) • *EdMar Lola*
	Bud: Cast-on stitch (page 73) • *EdMar Lola*
D	*Bud:* Straight stitch (page 83) • *Tapestry wool, perle #12*; Cast-on stitch (page 73) • *Perle #12*
E	*Calyx:* Cast-on stitch (page 73) • *Perle #8*
	Bud: Bullion knot (page 72), Straight stitch (page 83) • *Stranded cotton*
F	*Calyx:* Colonial knot (page 74) • *Crewel wool*
	Bud: Colonial knot (page 74) • *Stranded cotton*; Pistil stitch (page 80) • *Perle #12*
G	*Bud:* Straight stitch (page 83) • *Stranded cotton*
H	*Calyx:* Ribbon stitch (page 81) • *4mm silk ribbon*; Straight stitch (page 83) • *Stranded cotton*
	Bud: Lazy daisy stitch (page 79) • *4mm silk ribbon*; Straight stitch (page 83) • *Stranded cotton*
I	*Bud:* Straight stitch (page 83) • *Crewel wool*; Pistil stitch (page 80) • *Perle #8*
J	*Calyx:* Bullion knot (page 72) • *Perle #8*
	Bud: Lazy daisy stitch (page 79) • *Tulle thread*
K	*Calyx:* Cast-on stitch (page 73) • *Perle #8*
	Bud: Looped bullion knot stitch (page 80) • *Perle #8*; Straight stitch (page 83) • *Perle #12*
L	*Bud:* Looped cast-on stitch (page 80) with 2 needles; Straight stitch (page 83) • *Perle #8*
M	*Calyx:* Straight stitch (page 83) • *Stranded cotton*
	Bud: Bullion knot (page 72) • *Stranded cotton*
N	*Calyx:* Colonial knot (page 74) • *Perle #8*
	Bud: Ribbon stitch (page 81) • *4mm silk ribbon*; Straight stitch (page 83) • *7mm silk ribbon, stranded cotton*
	Stamens: Straight stitch (page 83) • *Stranded cotton*
O	*Calyx:* Ribbon stitch (page 81) • *4mm silk ribbon*
	Bud: French knot (page 78) • *7mm silk ribbon*
P	*Calyx:* Fly stitch (page 78), Straight stitch (page 83) • *Crewel wool*
	Bud: Single bead stitch (page 82) • *Nymo thread, beads*; French knot (page 78) • *Crewel wool*
Q	*Calyx:* Straight stitch (page 83) • *Perle #8*
	Bud: Lazy daisy stitch (page 79) • *4mm silk ribbon*
R	*Bud:* Lazy daisy stitch (page 79) • *Crewel wool*; Colonial knot (page 74) • *Perle #8*
S	*Bud:* Single bead stitch (page 82) • *Nymo thread, beads*

A
Calyx: Lazy daisy stitch (page 79), French knot (page 78) • *Crewel wool*

Bud: Ribbon stitch (page 81) • *4mm silk ribbon;* Straight stitch (page 83) • *Stranded cotton*

B
Calyx: Couching (page 74) • *4mm silk ribbon*

Bud: Ribbon loop stitch (page 81) • *4mm silk ribbon*

Leaves: Ribbon stitch (page 81) • *4mm silk ribbon*

C
Bud: Straight stitch (page 83) • *Perle #8;* Single bead stitch (page 82) • *Nymo thread, beads*

D
Calyx: Bullion knot (page 72) • *Crewel wool*

Bud: Tufting (page 84) • *Crewel wool*

E
Bud: Looped cast-on stitch (page 80), Straight stitch (page 83) • *Perle #12*

F
Bud: Ribbon loop stitch (page 81) • *4mm silk ribbon;* Single bead stitch (page 82) • *Nymo thread, beads*

G
Calyx: Ribbon stitch (page 81) • *4mm silk ribbon*

Bud: Beaded leaf (page 69) • *Nymo thread, beads*

H
Bud: Straight stitch (page 83) • *Tulle thread;* Couching (page 74) • *Crewel wool*

I
Calyx: Grab stitch (page 79) • *Crochet cotton*

Bud: Bullion lazy daisy stitch (page 72) • *EdMar Lola*

J
Calyx: Bullion knot (page 72) • *Crochet cotton*

Bud: Bullion knot (page 72), Straight stitch (page 83), Colonial knot (page 74) • *Perle #12*

K
Calyx: Cast-on stitch (page 73) • *Perle #8*

Bud: Drizzle stitch (page 76) • *Perle #12*

L
Calyx: Straight stitch (page 83) • *Crewel wool*

Bud: Straight stitch (page 83), Cast-on stitch (page 73), Colonial knot (page 74) • *Crewel wool*

M
Calyx: Bullion knot (page 72) • *Crewel wool*

Bud: Bullion knot (page 72), Colonial knot (page 74) • *Crewel wool*

N
Bud: Cast-on stitch (page 73) • *Perle #8;* Ribbon stitch (page 81) • *7mm silk ribbon*

7 Embroidery Stitches for Twigs

This is possibly my most favorite stage of the design process. The twigs add movement and dimension. It is important to keep your twigs fine and delicate; the choice of thread and color is very important. A finer thread will create a finer stitch.

A
Twigs: Straight stitch (page 83) • *Perle #8*
Buds: French knot (page 78) • *Crewel wool*

B
Twigs: Stem stitch (page 83) • *Perle #8*
Leaves: Lazy daisy stitch (page 79) • *Perle #8*

C *Twigs:* Couching (page 74) • *EdMar Lola*

D
Twigs: Straight stitch (page 83) • *Crewel wool*
Leaves: Lazy daisy stitch extended (page 79) • *Crewel wool*; Straight stitch (page 83) • *Stranded cotton*

E
Twigs: Chain stitch (page 74), Straight stitch (page 83) • *Perle #8*
Leaves: Lazy daisy stitch (page 79) • *4mm silk ribbon*
Buds: Single bead stitch (page 82) • *Nymo thread, beads*

F
Twigs: Backstitch (page 67) • *Metallic thread*; Single bead stitch (page 82) • *Nymo thread, beads*
Leaves: Lazy daisy stitch (page 79) • *Metallic thread*

G
Twigs: Twisted chain stitch (page 84) • *2mm silk ribbon*
Buds: Straight stitch (page 83), Colonial knot (page 74) • *Crewel wool*

H
Twigs: Backstitch (page 67), Straight stitch (page 83) • *Perle #8*
Buds: Straight stitch (page 83), Colonial knot (page 74) • *Perle #8*

I
Twigs: Couching (page 74), Fly stitch (page 78), Straight stitch (page 83) • *Crewel wool*
Twigs: Feather stitch (page 76) • *Crochet cotton*

J
Leaves: Straight stitch (page 83), Colonial knot (page 74) • *Crochet cotton*
Buds: Twisted lazy daisy stitch (page 84) • *Perle #8*

K
Twigs: Feather stitch (page 76) • *Crewel wool*
Buds: Straight stitch (page 83) • *Crewel wool*

L
Twigs: Feather stitch (page 76) • *Perle #8*
Leaves: Lazy daisy stitch (page 79) • *2mm silk ribbon*
Buds: Single bead stitch (page 82) • *Nymo thread, beads*

M
Twigs: Backstitch (page 67), Straight stitch (page 83) • *Perle #12*
Twigs: Stem stitch (page 83) • *Perle #12*

N
Leaves: Straight stitch (page 83) • *Perle #8*
Buds: Colonial knot (page 74) • *Perle #8*

O
Twigs: Twisted chain stitch (page 84), Straight stitch (page 83) • *Perle #8*

A
Twigs: Stem stitch (page 83) • *2mm silk ribbon*
Leaves: Straight stitch (page 83) • *Stranded cotton*

B
Twigs: Fern stitch (page 77) • *2mm silk ribbon*
Leaves: Straight stitch (page 83) • *Perle #12*

C
Twigs: Backstitch (page 67), Straight stitch (page 83) • *Crewel wool*
Leaves: Ribbon stitch (page 81) • *4mm silk ribbon*
Buds: Single bead stitch (page 82) • *Nymo thread, beads*

D
Twigs: Fly stitch (page 78) • *Perle #8*; Straight stitch (page 83) • *Stranded cotton*

E
Twigs: Fly stitch (page 78) • *Perle #8*
Leaves: Lazy daisy stitch (page 79) • *Perle #8*
Buds: Colonial knot (page 74) • *Perle #8*

F
Twigs: Stem stitch (page 83) • *Crewel wool*
Leaves: Straight stitch (page 83) • *Crewel wool*
Buds: Straight stitch (page 83), Colonial knot (page 74) • *Crewel wool*

G
Twigs: Feather twig stitch (page 76) • *Crewel wool*

H
Twigs: Backstitch (page 67), Whipping stitch (page 86) • *Perle #8*
Leaves: Lazy daisy stitch (page 79) • *4mm silk ribbon, perle #8, perle #12*; Straight stitch (page 83) • *Stranded cotton*

I
Twigs: Feather twig stitch (page 76) • *Perle #8*

J
Twigs: Feather twig stitch (page 76) • *2mm silk ribbon*

K
Twigs: Couching (page 74) • *Tapestry wool*; Straight stitch (page 83) • *Crewel wool*
Leaves: Ribbon stitch (page 81) • *4mm silk ribbon*
Buds: Single bead stitch (page 82) • *Nymo thread, beads*

L
Twigs: Stem stitch (page 83), Straight stitch (page 83) • *Perle #8*
Buds: Straight stitch (page 83) • *Tapestry yarn*

M
Twigs: Stem stitch (page 83), Straight stitch (page 83) • *Perle #8*
Leaves: Ribbon stitch (page 81) • *4mm silk ribbon*

N
Twigs: Backstitch (page 67) • *EdMar Frost*
Leaves: Single twisted chain stitch (page 82) • *EdMar Frost*

O
Twigs: Stem stitch (page 83), Straight stitch (page 83) • *Perle #8*
Leaves: Straight stitch (page 83) • *Perle #8*
Buds: Straight stitch (page 83), Lazy daisy stitch (page 79) • *Perle #12*

P
Twigs: Stem stitch (page 83), Straight stitch (page 83) • *Perle #12*

Q
Twigs: Stem stitch (page 83), Straight stitch (page 83) • *Crewel wool*
Buds: Colonial knot (page 74) • *Crewel wool*

I like to use beads sparingly; sprinkling them amongst embroidery adds light and movement to a floral design.

BEADING SAMPLER

A	*Flowers:* Beaded/couched sequin (page 68), Beaded backstitch (page 67) • *Nymo threads, beads*
	Stems: Portuguese knotted stem stitch (page 80), Stem stitch (page 83) • *Perle #12*
	Leaves: Beaded pointed petal/leaf (page 70) • *Nymo thread, beads*
B	*Center:* Beaded/couched sequin (page 68) • *Nymo thread, beads*
	Petals: Beaded rounded petal (page 71) • *Nymo thread, beads*
	Stem: Beaded backstitch (page 67) • *Nymo thread, beads*
	Leaves: Beaded backstitch (page 67) • *Nymo thread, beads*
C	*Center:* Beaded/couched sequin (page 68) • *Nymo thread, beads*
	Petals: Beaded backstitch (page 67) • *Nymo thread, beads*
D	*Center:* Single bead stitch (page 82) • *Nymo thread, beads*
	Petals: Beaded pointed petal/leaf (page 70) • *Nymo thread, beads*
E	*Flowers:* Beaded forget-me-not (page 69) • *Nymo thread, beads*
F	*Flowers:* Pistil stitch (page 80) • *Perle #12, sequins*
	Stem: Stem stitch (page 83) • *Perle #12*
G	*Bud:* Beaded lazy daisy stitch (page 69) • *Nymo thread, beads*
	Calyx: Beaded fly stitch (page 68) • *Nymo thread, beads*
H	*Flowers:* Beaded leaf (page 69) • *Nymo thread, beads*
	Stem: Stem stitch (page 83) • *Crochet cotton*
I	*Bud:* Single bead stitch (page 82) • *Nymo thread, beads*
	Calyx: Beaded fly stitch (page 68) • *Nymo thread, beads*
J	*Center:* Single bead stitch (page 82) • *Nymo thread, bead*
	Petals: Beaded lazy daisy stitch (page 69) • *Nymo thread, beads*
K	*Center:* Beaded/couched sequin (page 68) • *Nymo thread, beads*
	Petals: Beaded rounded petal (page 71) • *Nymo thread, beads*
L	*Flowers:* Beaded/couched sequin (page 68), Beaded lazy daisy stitch (page 69), Single bead stitch (page 82) • *Nymo thread, beads*
	Stem: Beaded backstitch (page 67) • *Nymo thread, beads*
M	*Flower:* Beaded daisy (page 68) • *Nymo thread, beads*
	Stem: Beaded backstitch (page 67) • *Nymo thread, beads*
	Leaves: Beaded leaf (page 69) • *Nymo thread, beads*
N	*Flowers:* Single bead stitch (page 82) • *Nymo thread, beads*
	Stem: Backstitch (page 67) • *Crewel wool*
	Leaves: Lazy daisy stitch (page 79) • *Crewel wool*
O	*Center:* Single bead stitch (page 82) • *Nymo thread, beads*
	Petals: Beaded backstitch (page 67) • *Nymo thread, beads*
	Stems: Couching (page 74) • *2mm silk ribbon*
	Leaves: Lazy daisy stitch (page 79) • *2mm silk ribbon*
P	*Flowers:* Beaded/couched sequin (page 68) • *Nymo thread, beads, sequins*; Single bead stitch (page 82) • *Nymo thread, beads*
	Stem: Thin stem stitch (page 83) • *Perle #12*
	Leaves: Beaded backstitch (page 67) • *Nymo thread, beads*

Silk ribbon is a glorious medium with which to embroider, sumptuous and so fulfilling.

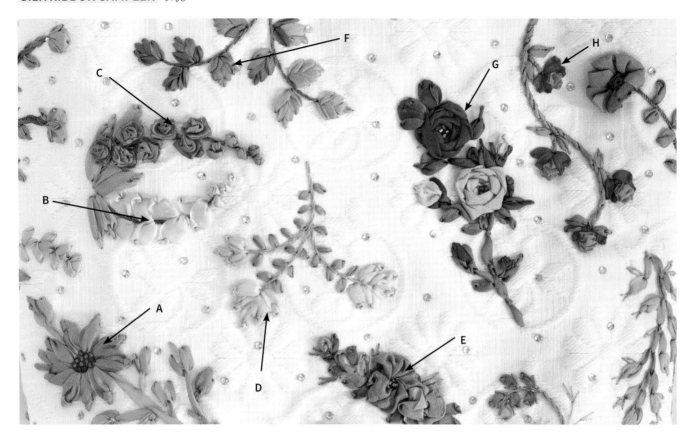

A
Center: Single bead stitch (page 82) • *Nymo thread, beads*

Petals: Lazy daisy stitch (page 79) • *7mm silk ribbon*

Stems: Couching (page 74) • *4mm silk ribbon*

Leaves: Fly stitch (page 78), Straight stitch (page 83) • *4mm silk ribbon*

Buds: Lazy daisy stitch (page 79), Fly stitch (page 78) • *4mm silk ribbon*

B
Petals: Ribbon stitch (page 81), French knot (page 78) • *7mm silk ribbon*

Stems: Stem stitch (page 83) • *Perle #8*

Leaves: Lazy daisy stitch (page 79) • *4mm silk ribbon*

C
Petals: Ruched rose (page 81), French knot (page 78) • *7mm silk ribbon*

Stems: Stem stitch (page 83) • *Perle #8*

Leaves: Lazy daisy stitch (page 79) • *4mm silk ribbon*

D
Petals: Knotted lazy daisy stitch (page 79) • *4mm silk ribbon*

Stems: Thin stem stitch (page 83) • *Twisted silk*

Leaves: Straight stitch (page 83) • *4mm silk ribbon*

E
Petals: Free-form flower with beaded center (page 78) • *13mm silk ribbon, Nymo thread, beads*

Leaves: Straight stitch (page 83) • *Perle #8*

Buds: Ribbon stitch (page 81), French knot (page 78) • *7mm silk ribbon*

F
Stems: Stem stitch (page 83) • *Perle #8*

Leaves: Fishbone stitch (page 77) • *4mm silk ribbon*

G
Center: Single bead stitch (page 82) • *Nymo thread, bead*

Petals: Spiderweb rose (page 82) • *7mm silk ribbon*

Stems: Couching (page 74) • *4mm silk ribbon*

Leaves: Ribbon stitch (page 81), Lazy daisy stitch (page 79) • *4mm silk ribbon*

Buds: Lazy daisy stitch (page 79), Fly stitch (page 78) • *4mm silk ribbon*

H
Petals: Ruched rose (page 81), Ribbon stitch (page 81) • *4mm silk ribbon*

Stem: Stem stitch (page 83) • *2mm silk ribbon*

Leaves: Lazy daisy stitch (page 79) • *4mm silk ribbon*

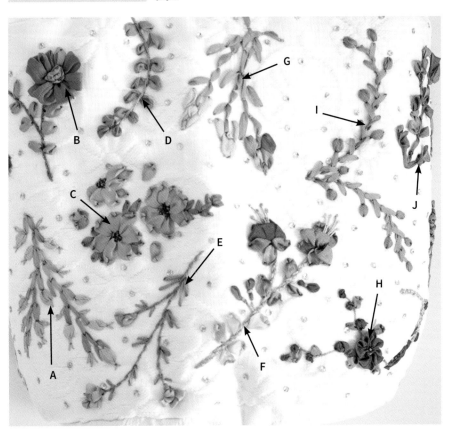

A
Stems: Feather stitch (page 76) • *4mm silk ribbon*

Leaves: Lazy daisy stitch (page 79) • *Stranded cotton*

Buds: Lazy daisy stitch (page 79) • *4mm silk ribbon*; Straight stitch (page 83) • *Stranded cotton*

B
Center: Ruched rose (page 81) • *7mm silk ribbon*

Petals: Ribbon loop stitch (page 81) • *7mm silk ribbon*

Stems: Stem stitch (page 83) • *Perle #8*

Leaves: Straight stitch (page 83) • *7mm silk ribbon*

C
Center: Single bead stitch (page 82) • *Nymo thread, bead*

Petals: Ribbon stitch (page 81) • *7mm silk ribbon*

Leaves: Ribbon stitch (page 81) • *7mm silk ribbon*

Buds: Ribbon stitch (page 81) • *4mm silk ribbon*

D
Petals: Straight stitch (page 83) • *7mm silk ribbon*

Stems: Thin stem stitch (page 83) • *Twisted silk*

Leaves: Straight stitch (page 83) • *7mm silk ribbon*

E
Petals: Ribbon loop stitch (page 81) • *4mm silk ribbon*

Calyx: Couching (page 74) • *4mm silk ribbon*

Stems: Thin stem stitch (page 83) • *Perle #12*

Leaves: Straight stitch (page 83) • *2mm silk ribbon*

F
Petals: Ribbon stitch (page 81), Ribbon loop stitch (page 81) • *7mm silk ribbon*

Stems: Portuguese knotted stem stitch (page 80) • *Perle #8*

Leaves: Ribbon stitch (page 81) • *7mm silk ribbon*

Buds: Straight stitch (page 83) • *7mm silk ribbon*; Couching (page 74) • *4mm silk ribbon*

Stamens: Pistil stitch (page 80) • *Stranded cotton*

G
Center: Colonial knot (page 74) • *4mm silk ribbon*

Petals: Lazy daisy stitch (page 79), Straight stitch (page 83) • *7mm silk ribbon*

Stems: Couching (page 74) • *4mm silk ribbon*

Leaves: Straight stitch (page 83) • *4mm silk ribbon*

H
Center: Free-form flower with beaded center (page 78) • *7mm silk ribbon, Nymo thread, bead*

Stems: Couching (page 74) • *Perle #12*

Leaves: Ribbon stitch (page 81) • *4mm silk ribbon*

Buds: French knot (page 78) • *4mm silk ribbon*

I
Petals: Straight stitch (page 83) • *4mm silk ribbon*

Stems: Twisted chain stitch (page 84) • *2mm silk ribbon*

J
Petals: Ribbon loop stitch (page 81) • *4mm silk ribbon*

Calyx: Straight stitch (page 83) • *4mm silk ribbon*

Stems: Couching (page 74) • *2mm silk ribbon*

Leaves: Ribbon loop stitch (page 81) • *4mm silk ribbon*

How to Start and Stop with Thread

Threading the Needle

Try "needling your thread" rather than "threading your needle"; by this I mean keep the thread still and move the needle onto the thread. Squeeze the end of the thread between thumb and forefinger and move the needle onto the thread as you slowly loosen the tension of the thumb and forefinger.

There is a large variety of needle threaders on the market from which to choose. Running the ends of the thread through a thread conditioner will tame any unruly fibers.

Knotting the Thread

1. Thread the needle.

2. Lay the knotting end of the thread over the needle.

3. Wrap the thread (clockwise) 2 or 3 times around the needle.

4. Hold the wraps between the thumb and forefinger and pull the thread through.

5. The wraps will close to form a knot.

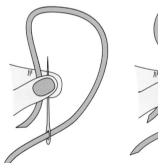  

Ending Off Threads

1. On the back of the work, take a small stitch from A to B; do not go through to the front of the work.

2. Pull the thread through until a small loop forms and slide the needle through.

3. Pull the thread through until another loop forms and slide the needle through.

4. Pull the thread firmly upwards until a small knot forms on the surface of the work.

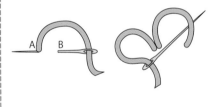 

How to Start and Stop with Silk Ribbon

Threading Silk Ribbon

1. Cut your ribbon into a 10″–12″ length.

2. Thread one end of the ribbon through the eye of the needle.

3. Turn the point of the needle and pierce the threaded end of ribbon.

4. Hold the point of the needle and pull the long end of the ribbon down, allowing the ribbon to "lock" over the eye.

Knotting Silk Ribbon

1. Make a ¼″ (6mm) fold at the end of the ribbon.

2. Pierce the fold with the point of the needle.

3. Pull it down over the needle to form a soft knot at the end.

Fastening Off Silk Ribbon

1. Use the blunt end of the needle to pass the ribbon under the back of a previously worked stitch.

2. Form a loop with the ribbon and pass the needle through the loop.

3. Gently pull the ribbon until the knot is tight.

Tip It is very important to keep the ribbon on the back of your work untwisted. This will allow the ribbon to fan out on the surface of your work.

Work with a loose tension when embroidering with silk ribbon.

Threading Brazilian Threads

1. There is a wrong and right end to the thread with Brazilian threads.

2. Gently twist the two ends together between your thumb and forefinger.

3. The end that unravels the most is the end to knot. The other end is the threading end.

Threading Crewel Wool

1. Fold the thread over the needle and apply some tension.

2. Hold the thread and slide the needle out of the folded thread.

3. Squeeze the thread tightly between thumb and forefinger and move the needle onto the thread as you slowly loosen the tension of the thumb and forefinger.

Alternating Stem Stitch

1. Working from left to right, bring the needle to the surface of the work at A.

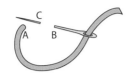

2. Insert the needle at B.

3. Emerge at C (midway between A and B), with the thread below the needle.

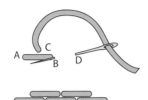

4. Work the following stitch in the same way, ensuring that the thread is above the needle.

5. Continue as desired, alternating the position of the thread, either above or below the needle.

Backstitch

1. Bring the thread to the surface of the work at A.

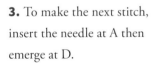

2. Take a small backward stitch at B and emerge at C.

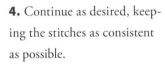

3. To make the next stitch, insert the needle at A then emerge at D.

4. Continue as desired, keeping the stitches as consistent as possible.

Beaded Backstitch

When securing a continuous line of beads, it is very important to follow this procedure.

1. Bring the needle to the surface of the work and pick up 3 beads.

2. Snug the beads up against each other and insert the needle into the fabric at the end of the third bead. Emerge between the first and second beads.

3. Travel through beads 2 and 3 and pick up 3 more beads.

4. Snug the beads up against each other and insert the needle at the end of the last bead.

5. Continue until the desired length is reached. Finish with an anchoring knot.

6. To straighten and smooth the line of beads, pass the needle and thread through the center length of beads, staying on the surface of the fabric. Once the end of the beading has been reached, insert the needle to the wrong side of the fabric and finish off.

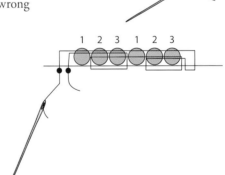

Beaded/Couched Sequin

1. Bring the needle to the surface of the work and pick up a sequin and seed bead.

2. Hold the seed bead between the thumb and index finger and reinsert the needle through the sequin.

3. The seed bead will now hold the sequin in place.

4. Finish with an anchoring knot on the wrong side of the fabric under the sequin before traveling along to the next sequin.

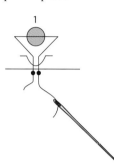

5. Alternative, a sequin *without a bead* can be simply couched down with a matching Nymo thread.

Beaded Daisy

1. Attach a round pearl bead to the fabric; this will form the center of the daisy.

2. Bring the needle to the surface of the work alongside the pearl bead.

3. Pick up 5 beads.

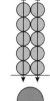

4. Insert the needle into the fabric and form an anchoring knot.

5. Repeat with another row of beads parallel to the first.

6. Emerge in the center of the parallel row of beads.

7. Pick up 1 round pearl bead and reinsert the needle within the parallel lines. This forms 1 petal of the daisy.

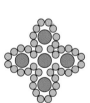

8. Continue until you have the desired number of petals for added detail.

Beaded Feather Stitch

1. Bring the needle to the surface of the work and pick up an even number of beads.

2. Allow the beads on the thread to form a V-shape.

3. Insert to the right of starting point at B.

4. With the needle over the thread, emerge at the bottom of the V (make sure that each side of the V has an equal number of beads) at C.

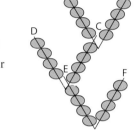

5. Repeat to the left.

6. Continue alternating from left to right for the desired length of feather stitching.

7. Finish with an anchoring knot.

Beaded Fly Stitch

1. Follow the instructions for Fly Stitch (page 78).

2. Pick up an even number of beads at Step 1.

3. Divide the beads to leave an even amount on either side of C.

4. Pick up the desired number of beads and reinsert the needle at D to form the anchor stitch.

Beaded Forget-Me-Not

The forget-me-not flower is made and then couched onto the surface of the work.

1. Thread a beading needle with approximately 12″ of Nymo beading thread. Pick up 6 pearl or round beads.

2. Pass the needle through the first 3 beads to form a circle with the thread.

> **NOTE**
> To finish with a center bead, continue to Step 3. To finish with a colonial knot, skip to Step 6.

3. Pick up a bead of a different color.

4. Pass the needle though the sixth pearl bead.

5. Pull both threads firmly so the center bead sits in the middle of the pearl beads.

6. Knot the threads tightly.

7. Use one of the threads and couch the flower to the surface of the work.

8. Pass the remaining thread to the back of the work and form an anchoring knot.

9. Make a colonial knot (page 74) using ribbon if no bead was added.

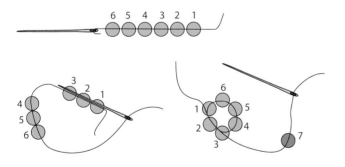

Couching

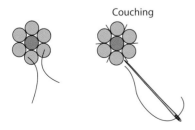

Beaded Lazy Daisy Stitch

1. Follow the instructions for Lazy Daisy Stitch (page 79).

2. Pick up an even number of beads at Step 1.

3. Divide the beads to leave an even amount on either side of C.

4. Pick up the desired number of beads and reinsert the needle at D to form the anchor stitch.

- -

Beaded Leaf

1. Bring the needle to the surface of the work at A and pick up 3 beads.

2. Insert the needle at B.

3. Bring the needle to the surface at C and pick up 3 beads.

4. Insert the needle at D, allowing the last 3 beads to form a gentle curve.

5. Finish with an anchoring knot.

Beaded Pointed Petal/Leaf

1. Bring the needle to the surface of the work and pick up 9 seed beads.

2. Hold the last bead you picked up (#9) between thumb and index finger.

3. Pass the needle through the next 2 beads (#8 and #7) on the thread.

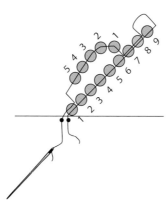

4. Pick up 5 beads and insert the needle into the fabric through the last bead (#1).

5. Finish with an anchoring knot on wrong side of fabric.

6. To anchor the petal, lay it flat on the surface of the work.

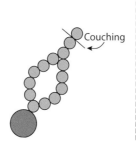

7. Bring the needle to the surface in line with the last bead (#9) of the petal.

8. Couch down by stitching over the beading thread of the petal.

9. Finish with an anchoring stitch.

Beaded Rose

1. Bring the needle to the surface at A and pick up 3 beads.

2. Insert at B.

3. Emerge at A and pick up 3 beads.

4. Insert at C.

5. Emerge at B, pick up 3 beads.

6. Insert at C.

7. Form an "ending off thread" (page 65) knot on the wrong side of the work.

8. Emerge at D and change the color of the beads.

9. Pick up 6 beads, insert at E, curving around the triangle.

10. Continue working around the triangle in this fashion.

11. Insert the last petal between D and the side of the central triangle of beads.

12. End off the thread (page 65) on the wrong side of the work.

13. Emerge at the center of the triangle and attach a single bead stitch (page 82) to complete the rose.

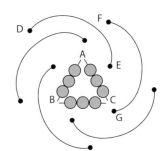

Beaded Rounded Petal

1. Bring the needle to the surface of the work and pick up 10 seed beads (increase the number of beads if a larger petal is desired, but always use an even number).

2. Insert the needle though the first picked-up bead and then into the fabric.

3. Form an anchoring knot on the wrong side of the fabric.

4. Lay the petal flat and emerge below the middle bead of the rounded petal.

5. Pass the needle through the middle bead and back down to the wrong side of the fabric. Finish with an anchoring stitch.

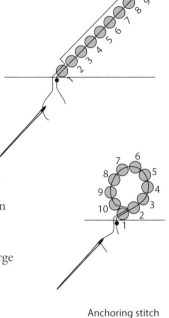

Anchoring stitch through bead

Beaded Stem Stitch

Follow the instructions for Stem Stitch (page 83). Use Nymo thread and pick up the desired number of beads for every stitch.

Beaded Tassel

1. Bring the needle to the surface of the work.

2. Pick up a combination of beads for desired length of tassel.

3. Hold the last bead between thumb and index finger and reinsert the needle through all other beads on the thread.

4. Finish with an anchoring knot. Add more strands as desired.

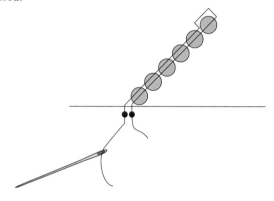

Blanket Stitch

1. Bring the needle to the surface of the work at A.

2. Insert the needle at B.

3. Emerge at C with the thread under the needle and pull the thread out of the work.

4. Continue as desired.

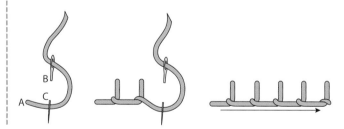

Bullion Knot

A milliners #1 or #3 needle must be used when forming a bullion knot.

1. Bring the needle to the surface of the work at A.

2. Insert at B (the distance between A and B will be the length of the bullion knot).

3. Emerge at A but do not pull your needle all the way through the fabric.

4. Wrap the working thread clockwise around the needle as many times as is required to equal the size of the backstitch.

5. Support the wraps on the needle with thumb and index finger and pull the needle through. Pull the thread away from and then toward you.

6. With the wraps evenly packed on the thread, reinsert needle at B to end the bullion knot.

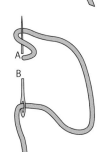
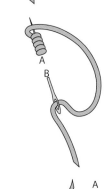

Bullion Lazy Daisy Stitch

1. Bring the needle to the surface of the work at A.

2. Make a loop with the thread/ribbon.

3. Hold the loop down with the nonworking hand, reinsert the needle where it first emerged at A, and emerge a short distance away at B.

4. Wrap the thread/ribbon clockwise around the needle 2 or 3 times.

5. Support the wraps on the needle and pull the needle through.

6. Insert at the tip of the bullion to anchor the stitch.

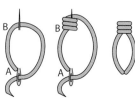

Bullion Rose Technique

A milliners #1 or #3 needle must be used when forming a bullion knot or cast-on stitch.

A cast-on stitch (next page) and/or bullion knot (at left) may be used in this technique to create roses.

1. Form a center for the rose in either bullion knots (at left), colonial knots (page 74), looped bullion knot stitch (page 80), looped cast-on stitch (page 80), or single bead stitch (page 82).

2. Emerge at A, insert at B, and emerge at A again, leaving the needle in the fabric.

3. Wrap the working thread clockwise around the needle as many times as is required to equal the size of the backstitch.

4. Support the wraps on the needle with thumb and index finger and pull the needle through. Pull the thread away from and then toward you.

5. With the wraps evenly packed on the thread, reinsert at B to end the knot.

6. To form the next bullion/cast on stitch, emerge at C, insert at D, and emerge at C again.

7. Continue stitching knots around the center, lengthening the knots as needed.

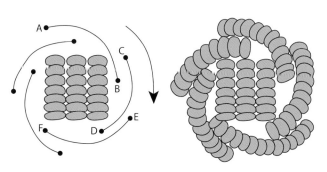

Cast-On Stitch

A milliner's #1 or #3 needle must be used when working a cast-on stitch.

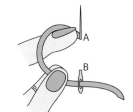

1. Bring the needle to the surface of the work at A and pull the thread through.

2. Insert the needle at the desired length for the stitch at B and emerge at A. Do not pull the needle through.

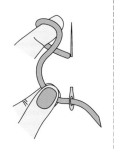

3. Hold the thread with your left thumb and middle finger approximately 3″ away from the surface of the work. Place your left index finger under the thread.

4. Rotate your left hand toward you in a clockwise direction and slip the loop off your index finger and onto the needle.

5. Pull the working thread toward you, sliding the knot down the needle onto the fabric.

6. Support the wraps on the needle with thumb and index finger and pull the needle through. Pull the thread away from and then toward you. Reinsert at B.

7. Take the needle through to the back of the work at B.

> **NOTE**
> To create a lacy effect to the stitch, loop over two needles instead of one.

Chain Feathered Stitch

1. Work a single chain stitch (page 74).

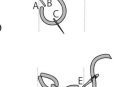

2. Insert the needle at D so that A-C-D forms a straight line.

3. Emerge at E which is at the angle of the previous line.

4. Work a single chain from E to D.

5. Insert at F so that E-D-F form a straight line.

6. Emerge at G which is at an angle to the previous line.

7. Continue as required. End with a small anchoring stitch.

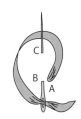

Chain Ribbon Stitch

1. Bring the thread to the surface of the work at A.

2. Insert the needle at B.

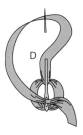

3. Emerge at C. With the ribbon under the needle, pull the ribbon though until a loop is formed. Do not pull too tightly as the loop will close.

4. Lay the ribbon flat on the surface of the work.

5. Insert the needle through the middle of the ribbon slightly ahead of the loop at C.

6. Loop the ribbon under the needle to form the next chain stitch.

7. Continue as desired.

Chain Stitch

1. Bring the needle to the surface of the work at A.

2. Loop the thread to the left and insert at B.

3. Emerge a short distance away at C and, with the thread under the needle, pull through.

4. Loop the thread to the left and insert the needle exactly where the thread emerged in the previous loop.

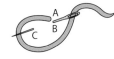

5. Continue as desired, finishing with a small anchoring stitch over the last loop.

Colonial Knot

1. Bring the thread to the surface of the work at A.

2. Cross the thread/ribbon over the needle from left to right. Wrap the thread/ribbon under the needle and then around the needle from right to left (creating a figure eight on your needle).

3. Reinsert the needle close to where it originally emerged.

4. Hold the needle in place and gently pull the working thread/ribbon taut toward the surface of your work. A firm knot is formed.

5. Pull the needle through to the back of the work.

Coral Stitch

1. Work from right to left to bring the thread/ribbon to the surface of the work at A.

2. Lay the thread/ribbon along the design line.

3. Secure the thread/ribbon with the left thumb of your nonworking hand.

4. Loop the thread/ribbon to the right and take a small stitch under the thread/ribbon from B to C.

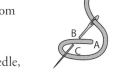

5. With the thread/ribbon under the needle, pull through.

6. Continue as desired.

7. To finish, stitch the thread/ribbon down on the wrong side of the work. The segments of thread/ribbon between the knots may be smooth or raised. The line formed may zigzag (pivoting at each point) or be curved or straight.

Couching

This technique is perfect for textured threads that cannot be drawn through the fabric. Experiment by using beads and contrasting threads for the couching stitch.

1. Lay a thread along the surface of your work.

2. Stitch it down with a series of small anchor stitches evenly spaced along the length of the laid thread.

Detached Blanket Stitch

1. Make a straight stitch (page 83) from A to B; the size of this foundation stitch will determine the finished stitch length.

2. Bring the needle to the surface of the work as close to A as possible.

3. Take the needle from the top to the bottom under the straight stitch (without piercing the fabric) with the thread under the needle.

4. Pull the thread through toward you, keeping the tension of the thread even and slightly relaxed.

5. Repeat until the foundation stitch is covered.

6. Take the thread through to the back of the fabric at B and end off.

NOTE

To make a leaf or petal, work 2 detached blanket stitches (above) parallel to each other. When taking the thread of the second detached blanket stitch through to the back of the work, insert the needle at the top of the first detached blanket stitch. This will create the point of the leaf or petal.

Detached Loop Stitch

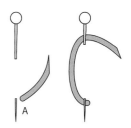

1. Insert a pin into the fabric; the distance between the entry and exit point will be the length of the complete detached loop stitch.

2. Bring the needle to the surface of the work at A.

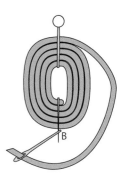

3. Take the thread under the pin and loop the thread around the pin.

4. Continue wrapping the thread as desired.

5. Insert the needle at B, which will be just under A.

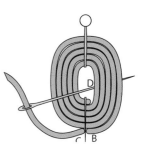

6. Reemerge at C, and staying on the surface of the work, wrap the needle around the base of the loop 2 or 3 times.

7. Remove the pin and secure the loops by inserting the needle at D.

Detached Twisted Chain Stitch

1. Bring the needle to the surface at A.

2. Insert the needle at B, level with A.

3. Emerge at C, twisting the thread over the needle and under the needle point.

4. Pull the thread through and form a long or short anchor stitch at D.

Drizzle Stitch

1. Bring the needle to the surface of the work at A.

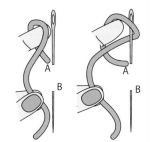

2. Insert at B which is as close to A as possible. Do not pull the needle out of the fabric.

3. Unthread the needle.

4. Hold the thread with your left thumb and middle finger approximately 3″ away from the surface of the work. Place your left index finger under the thread.

5. Rotate your left hand toward you in a clockwise direction and slip the loop off your index finger and onto the needle.

6. Pull the thread toward you, slipping the loops down the needle.

7. Continue as desired.

8. Rethread the needle.

9. Carefully pull the tip of the needle from the work at B but not at A.

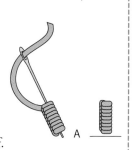

10. Pull the thread through to the back of the work at A, allowing the drizzle stitch to twist gently. Fasten off.

Feather Stitch

1. Bring the needle to the surface of the work at A.

2. Loop the thread/ribbon to the left and insert at B (in line with A).

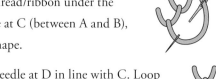

3. With the thread/ribbon under the needle, emerge at C (between A and B), forming a V-shape.

4. Insert the needle at D in line with C. Loop the thread/ribbon to the right and emerge at E.

5. Alternate the stitches from left to right. Continue as desired, finishing with a small anchor stitch over the last loop.

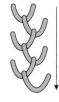

Feather Twig Stitch

This stitch is best worked away from you. It is possibly one of my favorite stitches to do.

1. Bring the needle to the surface of the work at A.

2. Insert at B, in line with A.

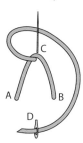

3. With the thread under the needle, emerge at C (between A and B), forming a V-shape. Pull the thread through.

4. With the thread to the left, insert the needle at D (in the middle and slightly lower than A and B).

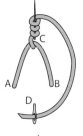

5. Emerge just above C.

6. Wrap the thread clockwise around the needle 2 or 3 times.

7. Support the wraps on the needle with thumb and index finger and pull the needle through, gently pushing the wraps toward C.

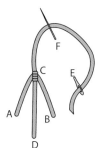

8. To form the next stitch, insert the needle at E (in line with C).

9. With the thread under the needle, emerge at F (between C and E), forming a V-shape. Pull the thread through.

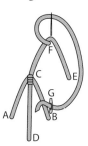

10. With the thread to the left insert the needle at G (in the middle and slightly lower than C and E).

11. Emerge just above F.

12. Wrap the thread clockwise around the needle 2 or 3 times.

13. Support the wraps on the needle with thumb and index finger and pull the needle through, gently pushing the wraps toward F.

14. Continue working the stitch, alternating left to right. Keep the thread to the left at all times.

Fern Stitch

1. Bring the needle to the surface of the work at A.

2. Insert at B and reemerge at A.

3. Insert at C and reemerge at A to complete the left-hand stitch.

4. Insert the needle at D and emerge at E to complete the right-hand stitch and set up for the next group. The 3 stitches that make up a fern stitch are usually the same length.

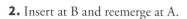

Fishbone Stitch

The fishbone stitch is the most versatile stitch to create leaves and petals.

1. Using an erasable pencil, draw a small leaf shape with a line down the center.

2. Begin at the tip of the leaf and make a straight stitch (page 83) from A to B.

3. Emerge at C, insert at D and emerge at E. Insert again at F.

4. Continue until the leaf shape is filled.

tip **Experiment with Different Threads, Beading, and Technique**

The tip of the fishbone stitch can be a straight stitch (page 83), lazy daisy stitch (page 79), lazy daisy stitch extended (page 79), or a twisted chain stitch (page 84).

Fishbone stitches:

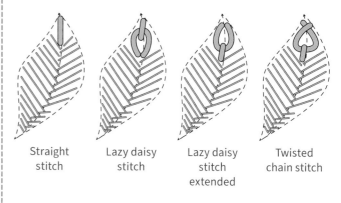

| Straight stitch | Lazy daisy stitch | Lazy daisy stitch extended | Twisted chain stitch |

Fishbone Stitch Variations

Fishbone Stitch: Open

Fishbone Stitch: Uneven Edge

Fishbone Stitch: Staggered

The vein of the staggered leaf is stitched first. Then apply the staggered fishbone stitches.

Fly Stitch

1. Bring the needle to the surface of the work at A.

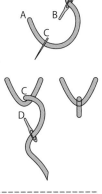

2. Insert at B and, with the thread/ribbon under the needle, emerge at C.

3. Insert at D to form the anchor stitch. The extended fly stitch has a longer anchoring stitch.

Free-Form Flower with Beaded Center

1. Thread a needle with a single strand of floss to match your silk ribbon of choice.

2. Make a knot at the end of the thread.

3. Start at one end of the ribbon; make small running stitches along the bottom edge.

4. Gather the ribbon to form a flower.

5. Stitch several times over the base of the flower so the flower can't pull out.

6. Stitch the flower to the desired background.

7. Use a single bead stitch (page 82) to add beads to the flower center.

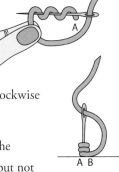

French Knot

1. Bring the needle to the surface of the work at A.

2. Wrap the thread around the needle one, two, or three times in a clockwise direction.

3. Holding the thread firmly, insert the needle at B (as close as possible to A, but not into A). Hold the knot in place until the needle is completely through the fabric.

Ghiordes Knot Stitch

When working with stranded cotton, separate each strand and then thread. This will allow the fibers to expand, creating a fluffy Ghiordes knot.

Create dimension by using different thicknesses and textures threaded through one needle.

The loops may be trimmed or left as loops. Ensure the stitches and loops are close together to create a fuller effect.

1. Insert the needle from the front of the work at A, leaving a tail on the surface of the fabric.

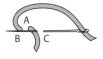

2. Emerge at B, to the left of A.

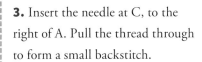

3. Insert the needle at C, to the right of A. Pull the thread through to form a small backstitch.

4. Reemerge at A, below the previous stitch.

5. Keeping the thread below the needle, insert at D, forming the first loop stitch.

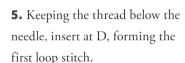

6. To form the next backstitch, reemerge at C and insert at E.

7. To form the next loop, insert the needle to the right of E.

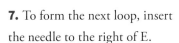

8. Continue as desired, ending with a tail on the surface of the fabric to match the first one.

When working in a circle, work from the outside to the inside.

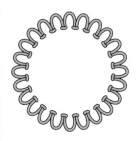

Grab Stitch

This stitch is simply a lazy daisy lying on its side with an extended anchoring stitch.

1. Bring the thread to the front of the work as close to the petal or flower as possible.

2. Form a lazy daisy, grabbing the base of the petal or flower.

3. Form a longer anchoring stitch to create a stem.

Herringbone Stitch

1. Bring the needle to the surface of the work at A.

2. Insert at B, diagonal to A.

3. Emerge at C, to the left of B.

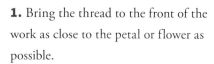

4. Insert at D, in line with A.

5. Emerge at E, to the left of D.

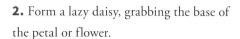

6. Continue as desired.

Knotted Lazy Daisy Stitch

Follow the instructions for Lazy Daisy Stitch (above right). Replace the anchoring stitch at C with a French knot (previous page).

Lazy Daisy Stitch

1. Bring the needle to the surface of the work at A.

2. Make a loop with the thread/ribbon.

3. Hold the loop down with the nonworking hand, reinsert the needle where it first emerged at B, and emerge a short distance away at C.

4. With the thread/ribbon under the needle, make a small stitch from C to D to anchor the loop.

Lazy Daisy Stitch Extended

Follow the instructions for Lazy Daisy Stitch (above) and extend the anchoring stitch to the desired length.

Lazy Daisy Stitch with Bead

1. Follow the instructions for Lazy Daisy Stitch, Steps 1–3 (above).

2. Pick up the desired of beads on the needle and complete Step 4.

Looped Bullion Knot Stitch

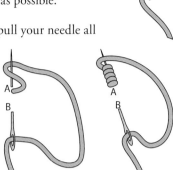

1. Bring the needle to the surface of the work at A.

2. Insert at B, as close to A as possible.

3. Emerge at A but do not pull your needle all the way through the fabric.

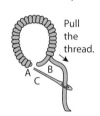

4. Wrap the working thread around the needle as many times as required, creating a loop.

5. Support the wraps on the needle with thumb and index finger and pull the needle through. Pull the thread away from and then toward you.

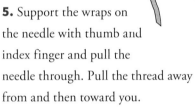

6. With the wraps evenly packed on the thread, insert the needle at C and end the looped bullion knot stitch.

Looped Cast-On Stitch

The looped cast-on stitch is worked in the same way as a cast-on stitch (page 73). The only difference is the size of the "bite" of fabric between A and B is as small as possible.

Palestrina Knot Stitch

1. Working horizontally, bring the needle to the surface of the fabric at A, insert at B, and emerge at C.

2. Without going through the fabric, pass the needle under the straight stitch (between A and B) and pull through gently, keeping the stitch loose.

3. Pass the needle under the straight stitch (between A and B), keeping the previous stitch and the looped thread under the needle. Pull through.

4. Continue as desired, spacing the knots by taking another small stitch at D and E to repeat.

Pistil Stitch

> **NOTE**
> To secure a sequin with a pistil stitch, simply place the sequin on the surface of the work at B. Wrap the thread around the needle and reinsert in the center of the sequin to secure in place.

1. A pistil stitch is a straight stitch (page 83) with an attached French knot (page 78).

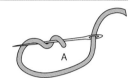

2. Bring the needle to the surface of work at A and wrap the thread around the needle 2 or 3 times. Hold the thread taut and insert at B. Pull the needle though.

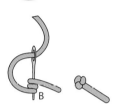

Portuguese Knotted Stem Stitch

1. Bring the needle to the surface of the work at A, insert the needle at B, and emerge at C.

2. Pull the thread firmly, and slide the needle under the stem stitch just made below C.

3. Slide the needle under the same stitch at C, below the first coil. Gentle push the coils up to C.

4. Create another stem stitch and slide the needle twice under the first and second stem stitch.

5. Continue as desired.

Ribbon Loop Stitch

1. Bring the ribbon to the surface of the work at A.

2. Make a tiny backstitch and insert at B.

3. Place a pencil or straw through the ribbon loop and, keeping the ribbon untwisted, gently pull the ribbon over the pencil or straw. Remove the pencil or straw once the ribbon is taut.

4. Repeat for the next loop stitch. Secure the ribbon on the wrong side of the work to end.

5. To make a loop stitch flower, mark a small circle with an erasable pencil where the flower center will be.

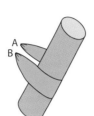

6. Make a series of loop stitch petals around the outside of the marked circle.

7. Work clockwise, keeping the back of the marked circle clear of any silk ribbon.

8. Add colonial knots (page 74) or beads to the center of the flower.

Ribbon Stitch

1. Bring the ribbon to the surface of the work at A.

2. Lay the ribbon flat and insert the needle through the ribbon where you want the tip of the stitch to be.

3. Pull the ribbon gently through the work. The ribbon will curl inwards to form a point (be careful not to pull too tightly).

4. Secure the ribbon on the wrong side of the work to end.

Rope Stitch

1. Bring the needle to the surface of the work at A.

2. Insert the needle at B immediately below A.

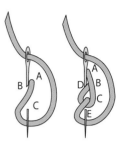

3. Form a loop with the thread and emerge at C, directly below B and inside the loop, creating a twisted chain stitch (page 84).

4. Insert the needle at D into the divot formed by the previous twisted chain stitch.

5. Form a loop with the thread and emerge at E.

6. Continue as desired.

Ruched Rose

1. Bring the ribbon to the surface of the work.

2. Hold the ribbon in the nonworking hand approximately 3″ away from the surface of work. Form a colonial knot (page 74).

3. Keeping the knot on the needle, form small gathering stitches along the length of the ribbon.

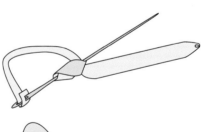

4. Once the end of the ribbon has been reached, insert the needle into your work close to where it emerged.

5. Gently pull the ribbon through.

6. A small rose will form.

7. Secure the ribbon on the wrong side of the work to end.

tip A variegated silk ribbon will give your rose shading without you having to change the ribbon during the stitching of it.

Single Bead Stitch

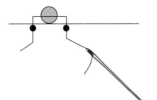

1. When attaching a single bead of any size, bring the thread from the back to the front.

2. Put the bead on the needle and insert the needle into the fabric to the back of the work. Form an anchoring knot to end.

Single Twisted Chain Stitch

Follow the instructions for Twisted Chain Stitch (page 84), except twist the chain stitch only on one side, either left or right.

Spanish Knotted Feather Stitch

This stitch may seem confusing at first. It may be helpful to know that it is made up of a series of twisted chains.

1. Bring the thread to the surface of the work at A.

2. Hold the thread to the left.

3. Insert the needle at B and emerge at C.

4. Pull the thread through with the thread under the needle to form a twisted chain.

5. Insert the needle in the center above the twisted chain at D.

6. Take a starting stitch to emerge at E.

7. Pull the thread through with the thread under the needle to form another twisted chain.

8. Continue working twisted chains, alternating from left to right.

Spiderweb Rose

1. With an erasable pencil, mark a temporary circle with 5 evenly spaced spokes.

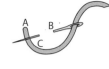

2. With a single strand of coordinating thread, make a fly stitch (page 78) to create the first 3 spokes and then a straight stitch (next page) for the other 2 spokes.

3. Bring the ribbon/thread to the surface of the work at the center of the spokes.

4. Without piercing the fabric or ribbon/thread, weave the ribbon/thread over and under the spokes, allowing the ribbon/thread to twist. Keep the weave soft and loose.

5. Continue until the rose is full.

6. Take the ribbon/thread to the back of the work and end off.

7. Add seed beads or colonial knots (page 74) for the rose center.

Spiderweb Rose Variation

1. Mark the desired size center for the spiderweb rose.

2. Work an uneven number of evenly spaced straight stitches around the marked center.

3. Bring the needle to the surface of the work alongside one spoke.

4. Weave the needle over and under the spokes until all are covered.

5. Take the ribbon/thread to the back of the work and end off.

6. Add colonial knots, beads, or any desired stitch to create the center.

Stem Stitch

This stitch works from left to right as you keep the thread or ribbon either above or below the needle.

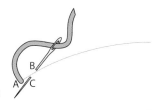

1. Bring the needle to the surface of the work at A. Insert at B.

2. Emerge at C, halfway between A and B.

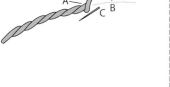

3. Continue stitching a half-stitch forward, keeping the thread either above or below the needle throughout.

Stem Stitch Rose

1. Make a center for the rose using colonial knots (page 74), single bead stitch (previous page), beaded/couched sequin (page 68), or your stitch of choice.

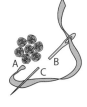

2. Bring the needle to the surface of the work at A.

3. Insert at B and emerge at C, keeping the thread below the needle.

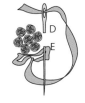

4. Insert at D and emerge at E.

5. Continue working in a circular pattern to complete the rose. Keep the tension of the ribbon relaxed.

Stem Stitch with Beads

To add texture to a stem stitch (above), simply pick up a bead on every second stitch.

Straight Feather Stitch

1. Bring the needle to the surface of the work at A.

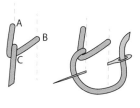

2. Loop the thread to the right and insert the needle at B.

3. Emerge at C, in line with A, and pull the thread through in a downward direction.

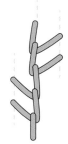

4. Make a second stitch in this way.

5. To change to the left, loop the thread to the left and repeat Steps 2 and 3.

6. Continue as desired.

Straight Stitch

This simple stitch, sometimes called a *stab stitch*, is so versatile! I use it with gay abandon, creating leaves, stems, pistils, you name it! When working with silk ribbon, twist it once or twice between A and B.

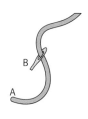

1. Bring the needle to the surface of the work at A.

2. Work a stitch to B in the required length and direction.

Thin Stem Stitch

Follow the instructions for Stem Stitch (above left), the only difference being that the "bite" of the fabric is smaller and the stitch is longer.

Thorn Stitch

Experiment with contrasting threads with this easy and effective stitch.

1. Begin with a long straight stitch (page 83) to form the foundation for your "thorns."

2. Bring the needle to the surface of the work at A.

3. Insert at B, crossing and close to the foundation stitch.

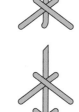

4. Emerge at C, opposite A.

5. Insert at D, opposite B.

6. Emerge at E, in line with A.

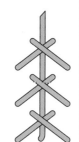

7. Continue along the length of the foundation stitch.

Tufting

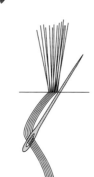

1. Separate 12 strands of stranded cotton. Thread a needle with all 12 strands.

Holding stitch

2. Insert the needle into the surface of the work, leaving a tail of strands at least as long as the desired tuft.

3. Turn to the back of the work and complete a small holding stitch in the backing fabric.

4. Turn to the front of the work and bring the needle to the surface very close to where the needle went down.

Cut.

5. Holding all the strands firmly together, cut them to the desired length to form the tuft.

Twisted Chain Stitch

1. Bring the needle to surface of the work at A.

2. Loop the thread to the right and insert at B.

3. With the thread under the needle, emerge at C, under A.

4. Loop the thread to the left and insert at D.

5. With the thread under the needle, emerge at E.

6. Loop the thread to the right and insert at F.

7. With the thread under the needle, emerge at G.

8. Repeat for the desired length, alternating the stitch form left to right.

9. Finish with a small stitch over the last chain.

Twisted Lazy Daisy Stitch

1. Bring the needle to the surface of the work at A.

2. Insert the needle at B.

3. Emerge at C, twisting the thread over the needle and under the needle tip.

4. Pull the thread through and make an anchor knot at the desired length.

Uneven Chain Stitch

1. Bring the needle to the surface of the work at A and pull the thread through.

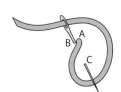

2. Insert the needle at B, slightly to the left of A. Go down at B and up again at C in one movement. Keep the needle in the fabric.

3. Form a "twisted loop" with the thread, ensuring that the thread lies across the needle.

4. Pull the thread through.

5. To form a new uneven chain, insert the needle at D slightly in front of the previous chain; repeat.

6. Continue to the desired length.

Up-and-Down Blanket Stitch

1. Begin as you would an ordinary blanket stitch (page 71).

2. Insert the needle at D and emerge at E with the thread under the needle.

3. Pull the thread out of the work in an upward movement, then downward to bring the 2 stitches into position.

4. Continue as desired.

Upright Rose Technique

Start at the top and work downward using the desired stitch.

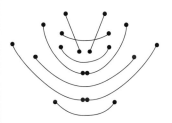

Wheatear Stitch

1. Work 2 straight stitches (page 83) at A and B, and then C and D.

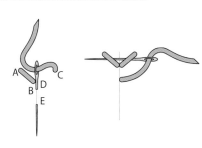

2. Bring the thread through below these stitches at E.

3. Pass the needle under the 2 straight stitches without entering the fabric.

4. Insert at F.

5. Emerge at G to begin the next series of stitches.

Whipping Stitch

A whipping stitch is where a second thread is worked over a foundation line of another stitch.

1. Work a line of a chosen foundation stitch.

2. Bring the whipping thread to the surface of the fabric to the left of the foundation stitch.

3. Slide the eye end of the needle under the first stitch of the foundation row of stitches.

4. Keep the tension of the whipping thread relaxed.

5. Continue down the length of the foundation stitch.

Woven Bar

1. Insert a pin into the fabric; the distance between the entry and exit point will be the length of the completed woven bar.

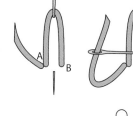

2. Bring the needle to the surface of the work at A.

3. Take the thread around the pin and insert at B, and bring the needle back out to the left of A.

4. Weave the needle over the left spoke and under the right spoke.

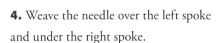

5. Pull the thread through and push the wrap down toward A and B.

6. Weave the needle over the right spoke and under the left spoke.

7. Continue weaving until the spokes are firmly packed.

8. Take the needle to the back of the work at the tip of the woven bar.

Woven Picot

1. Insert a pin into the fabric; this will be the length of the picot.

2. Bring the needle to the surface of the work at A.

3. Take the thread around the pin head, insert at B and emerge at C. Pull the thread through.

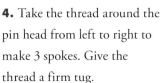

4. Take the thread around the pin head from left to right to make 3 spokes. Give the thread a firm tug.

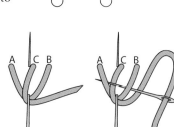

5. Working from right to left, weave the thread under the right-hand spoke, over the center spoke, and under the left-hand spoke.

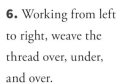

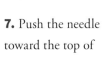

6. Working from left to right, weave the thread over, under, and over.

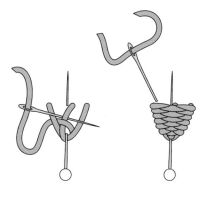

7. Push the needle toward the top of the picot.

8. Continue weaving from side to side, taking care not to pull the side of the picot in.

9. Pack the rows as tightly as possible.

10. Remove the pin and reinsert the needle at A and end off the thread on the wrong side of the work.

Woven Spiderweb

1. With an erasable pencil, draw a circle the size you want the finished web. Use a straight stitch (page 83) to make 8 evenly spaced spokes from A to B, C to D, E to F, and G to H.

2. Bring the needle to the surface of the work in the center of 2 spokes, and straight stitch (page 83) across the center of the spokes.

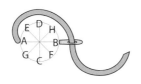

3. Bring the needle to the surface of the work, near the center and between the 2 stitches. Without piecing the fabric, go over the spoke to the right and then under it, and then under the next spoke to the left.

4. Pull your thread toward the center.

5. Go back over the spoke you just went under, and then under it and under the next spoke to the left.

6. Continue working counter-clockwise until the desired fullness has been reached. You are wrapping the thread around each spoke as you go.

7. Finish with a small anchor stitch on the wrong side of the work. A partial spiderweb can also be worked over 5 stitches.

Gallery

Collection of embroidery works

Embroidered Clutch

Embroidered Pin Cushion

Embroidered Needle Case

Embroidered Teddy Bear

Embroidered Sewing Roll

Repurposed Fabric and Embroidered Collage

Repurposed Wool and Embroidered Quilt

Free-form embroidery

Embroidered Woolen Bag

Embroidered Fabric Collage

Snippets and embroidery

Autumn Leaves

About the Author

Jennifer Clouston is a textile artist, third-time author, and sought-after tutor. After being introduced to quilting in South Africa in 1988, Jennifer quickly discovered that handwork, rather than sitting at a sewing machine, was her true passion. The combination of embroidery, hand piecing, and quilting led her to crazy quilting, a pivotal moment in her quilting life. In a process that begins with freedom and play, Jennifer found a creative outlet that saw her fusing the influences of her childhood in South Africa with the traditions of Victorian crazy quilting.

Jennifer's trademark is a modern and playful take on traditional embroidery. This has provided inspiration both in her classes and published books, the top seller *Foolproof Crazy Quilting* and *Foolproof Crazy-Quilt Projects*. Preferring a freehand approach to embroidery, Jennifer designs new and original stitches by taking traditional embroidery stitches and giving them a modern twist. With the help of her husband, Vaughn, who draws and brings to life new patterns and stitch dictionaries as well as her books, she is able to share her fresh and original approach.

Jennifer's goal is to encourage fellow quilters and stitchers to take risks and create from their own individuality and uniqueness; to continue relishing this cherished tradition by making embroidery accessible, producing work that can be used in day-to-day life. This inspiration encourages play and exploration within the four walls of the sewing room.

Photo by Ainslie Clouston

Visit Jennifer online and follow on social media!

Website: jenniferclouston.com

Blog: sewsocrazy.blogspot.com

Instagram: @jennifer_clouston_embroidery

- -

Also by Jennifer Clouston:

Bibliography

One Hundred/100 Embroidery Stitches.
Coats & Clark Inc., 1964.

A–Z of Embroidery Stitches. Search Press, 2014.

Erica Wilson's Embroidery Book.
Charles Scribner's Sons, 1973.